CHINESE ASTROLOGY FOR 2019

FOR

2019

THE YEAR OF THE EARTH PIG

豬

己亥

年運程上卷

己
亥
年

The Year of the Earth Pig

Chinese Astrology for 2019

All intellectual property rights including copyright in relation to this book belong to Joey Yap Research Group Sdn. Bhd.

JOEY YAP RESEARCH GROUP SDN BHD (944330-D)
19-3, The Boulevard, Mid Valley City,
59200 Kuala Lumpur, Malaysia.
Tel   : +603-2284 8080
Fax   : +603-2284 1218
Email   : info@masteryacademy.com
Website   : www.masteryacademy.com

DISCLAIMER:

INDEX

己亥年

The Year of the Earth Pig

PREFACE

Towards the end of the year, we invariably start to think about the future. I am often approached by people who want to know whether the new year will be good or bad for them. People who have experienced heartbreak, loss or injury frequently wonder if the coming year will be easier. Others have more specific questions about what the new year will bring in terms of their career, business, marriage and social life.

Traditional Chinese Astrology gives us the power to answer these questions. I published the first incarnation of this book on Chinese Astrology way back in 2006. In the years since, interest in the subject has continued to grow and grow, and the positive reviews have kept coming.

Most people know that Chinese Astrology focuses on the twelve animal signs. With a traditional forecast, results are ultimately based on the year that a person was born. What is less well known is that animal sign forecasting is actually a form of BaZi Destiny analysis.

The word BaZi means "Eight Characters" and in a full BaZi reading, one must analyse all Eight Characters in a person's chart. Together, they paint a complete picture of that person's destiny. In BaZi, everyone has a Destiny chart which is derived from the Year, Month, Day and Hour of their birth.

Forecasting using a person's animal sign alone (which is assigned by the Year of birth) only makes use of 12.5% of a BaZi chart. By using more of a BaZi chart, we can draw more accurate and tailored conclusions. A large section of this book focuses on how to analyse the Day Pillar or Jia Zi (甲子) in a person's BaZi chart. You won't find this feature in any other book and it can make a big difference to your forecasts.

I've studied Chinese Metaphysics and provided BaZi consultancy services for over two decades now. I can say with complete confidence that there is no such thing as a truly good or bad year. We are not helpless with regards to the future. To make the point, imagine if a person's outlook for the year ahead was favourable but they chose to spend the entire year on the sofa. What would come of their good fortune? Very little! The importance of mindset and effort should not be underestimated. Conversely, if a person's outlook is poor, they must not be deterred. With adequate preparation, we can always minimize hardship and loss and come out on top. Equally, knowing that an opportunity is coming let us prepare for it and make the most out of it.

It is important to stress that even with the techniques herein, an astrology reading can really only offer a glimpse into the future. The gold standard for Destiny analysis will always be a professional BaZi consultation, because Destiny analysis is inherently complex and nuanced. From there, Feng Shui and Qi Men Dun Jia can help one act on what they learn. If BaZi can provide the diagnosis, then Feng Shui and Qi Men Dun Jia are like the prescription!

With all that being said, you can still significant insight into the year ahead with the help in this book. Nonetheless, it should still provide a useful analysis on the yearly general prospects for you. Knowledge really is power, and with the right attitude and information you can make 2019 the very best year it can possibly be.

Whatever the future may hold for you, I wish you good luck!

Warmest regards,

Dato' Joey Yap
July 2018

Connect with us:

www.joeyyap.com   JOEYYAP TV www.youtube/joeyyap

@DatoJoeyYap   @RealJoeyYap   @JoeyYap

Academy website:
www.masteryacademy.com I jya.masteryacademy.com I www.baziprofiling.com

The Earthly Branches

In BaZi, the Earthly Branches on the BaZi Chart consist of the Four Pillars namely, the Hour, Day, Month and Year Pillars, as illustrated below. You need to refer to the forecast of each of the Animal Sign that appears on the respective Pillars of your BaZi Chart in order to derive a more comprehensive outlook for the year.

Each Pillar signifies a different aspect in life:

Internal Your inner personality and behaviour that are hidden from and not openly revealed to others.		External The personality and behaviour you exhibit outwardly and can be seen by others.	
Hour Pillar denotes a person's dreams, hopes and inspirations.	**Day Pillar** represents an individual's relationship with his or her spouse.	**Month Pillar** reveals one's career and business outlook.	**Year Pillar** shows a person's state of health and social circle (i.e. friends).

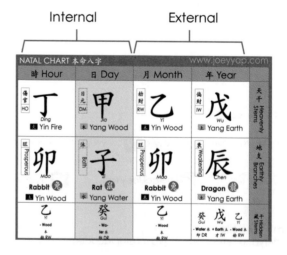

Do This First

Print your Free BaZi Chart at the URL below:

www.masteryacademy.com/regbook

Here is your unique code to access the BaZi Calculator:

CA12BZ68

Sample: This is how your BaZi Chart will look like

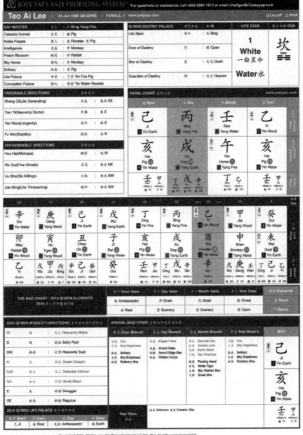

Exclusive content available for download with your purchase of the Chinese Astrology for 2019 book.

Claim your FREE ONLINE ACCESS now at:
www.masteryacademy.com/bookbonus2019

BONUS CONTENT

FREE
DOWNLOAD

CAR92AC6

Expires
31st December 2019

The Year of the Earth Pig Outlook

The coming year of the Earth Pig, Ji Hai 己亥 will be one of sluggishness but sure growth and development in many areas. On a global scale, political failures will catalyze social change. The technology, entertainment, oil and gas industries are all expected to flourish. On a personal scale, there may be some difficulties, particularly for those who plan on getting married.

Without further ado, here's what 2019 has in store for us.

2018 was a year of tremendous geopolitical and economic change. Many of the events that took place in 2018 will create new opportunities in 2019. However, to profit from these opportunities, new governments, policies and commercial infrastructure will have to put in place. Consequently, some sectors will only flourish in the second half of the year after experiencing a slow start.

Behind closed doors, 2019 will bring about different political priorities and ideas, but it may not be easy to see the forces of change at work. The discord will be largely hidden from the general public as officials try to present a brave face. This is akin to the way a hidden fire can slowly boil away water. There will be increased geopolitical tension, fraught trade negotiations and even conflict between administrative power houses and countries in the South and West. On a more positive note, there will be some progress in religious relations and tensions will ease. We can infer all of this from the presence of the Stem Ji 己 Earth which suggests stability while the Branch Hai 亥 (Pig) hints at internal instability and impatience.

The general public will feel a growing sense of dissatisfaction towards their government, who will appear increasingly unable to solve the problems they are faced with. This will motivate people in the workforce to take matters into their own hands. People – not their governments - will drive new developments and better policy implementation. This is evident from the way the Shen 申 (Monkey) and Yin 寅 (Tiger) in the chart Clash with one another, representing widespread dissatisfaction. Ren 壬 Water represents the people, arbitrating the aforementioned Clash and taking matters into their own hands.

Big players in industry will join forces to keep the economy moving. The Year of the Earth Pig will be one of new government alliances, economic collaborations, mergers and treaties. All of this will help improve the country's economic prospects. These assertions are supported by the combination of Hai 亥 (Pig) and Yin 寅 (Tiger), representing the economy and the government respectively.

In the Year of Earth Pig, people will become even more connected. The social media industry will grow even larger as more people log on and the tech giants collaborate on new platforms. The Fire element will be particularly bright and influential in 2019, which tells us to expect innovations and breakthroughs in the world of tech.

In 2018, Hollywood and the entertainment industry were rocked by allegations of misconduct. In 2019, new scandals will break. Because of the influence of the Fire element, rumour and scandal will be able to spread with ferocious speed, like a raging wildfire!

Unfortunately for those involved in the Malaysian property market, 2019 will likely see stagnated growth with little to no movement relative to 2018. This is due to the way the intense Fire element causes the Earth element to become dry and rigid.

The financial sector won't fare much better. The rate of inflation is expected to rise further, slowing demand for precious metals. The generally abrupt financial outlook for 2019 can be attributed to the weakness of the Metal element and the clash between Metal and Wood in the chart overall.

The agricultural industry should brace itself for one or more natural disasters, stunting growth thereafter. The most likely natural disaster is flooding which is a possibility across the globe. That's because Fire is the strongest element in the 2019 BaZi chart and it has the ability to "melt" ice, turning it into volumes of water. It can also blaze through the Wood element.

Fans of space exploration can look forward to major new discoveries about our solar system in 2019, as indicated by the Year Branch Hai 亥 (Pig). The space probes that will likely make these discoveries are actually already in situ.

On a personal level, the Year of the Earth Pig will be characterized by minor setbacks for some and drastic changes for others – particularly those looking to tie the knot! This could mean a change of wedding venue, issues with the in laws or completely rescheduling because of inauspicious dates. To maintain control, you may need to develop multiple backup plans and think on your feet. The year 2019 may also see arguments with in-laws, so it may be wise to minimize your interactions with them. Alternatively, you may be able to keep the peace by showing them more empathy.

Watch out for digestive viral illness in 2019. Ji Hai 己亥 represents Muddy Water, which symbolizes virus, outbreaks of diseases and problems with the digestive system. You should also keep an eye out for issues affecting the reproduction system, urinary tract and bladder, which are all represented by Hai 亥 (Pig). If you notice any changes in your body, the best thing to do is speak to a doctor at the earliest opportunity.

Sadly, there will be more accidents than normal on the roads in 2019. The presence of the Three Growth Stars, combined with a Clash between two of the Growth Stars Shen 申 (Monkey) and Yin 寅 (Tiger) in the BaZi Chart means that there is a greater chance of transportation related crashes. Stay vigilant behind the wheel and where possible, give other drivers a wide berth and make sure you have renewed your insurance.

As 2018 draws to a close, there is lots to look forward to in the year of the Earth Pig. With insight into the year ahead, you can better prepare for the events that may affect you, your family or business. Whatever challenges may be coming your way in 2019, I believe this guide can help you overcome them and make 2019 a year to remember! I wish you good luck.

Forecast for the 12 Animal Signs in 2019

Pig 亥

Year of the Pig							
1923	1935	1947	1959	1971	1983	1995	2007

A person's Chinese age is obtained by adding one year to their Western birthday. For example, if you were born in 1976, your Western age in 2019 is 43, but your Chinese age would be 44.

Overall Forecast For The Year

Happiness in life comes from being able to handle challenges and making the best out of any situation. This year will be a good test for you; remember that no problem is too big to overcome if you don't give up. You have just the right Star on your side to help you find ways to resolve conflicts. How you handle your relationships with others will also define your new year; if you can stay focused on what's important and not allow others to distract you from your goals, you will get through this eventful year with flying colours.

The presence of the Relief God Star (解神) is the silver lining to your new year, as it gives you the ability to mitigate the worst effects of the negative Stars in your chart. This Star will help you find solutions and untangle yourself from difficulties. When in doubt, take the time to look within yourself as most of the time, you will realize that you hold all the keys to resolve the issues dwelling in your heart. Once you let go of unnecessary pride and stubbornness, you will find yourself free to turn your life around.

Pig individuals with a thirst for knowledge will find much to like about this year. With the blessing of the Eight Seats Star (八座), you will have an enhanced capacity for learning and self-development. This the perfect year to sign up for that course to enhance your skills or take your hobbies to the next level. This Star also ensures that you will find ample support from Noble People around you and have unexpected opportunities for personal advancement. It will be advantageous for you to keep an open mind, stay curious and say yes whenever there is an opportunity to learn something new.

With the presence of the Back Poking Star (指背) and the Hidden Corpse Star (伏屍), you may reluctantly find yourself being caught in squabbles and arguments in your work and personal relationships. Office conflicts usually stem from malicious gossip and jealousy from colleagues. Instead of allowing other people to affect your work performance, try to stay calm and focused on what truly matters. On the home front, there are buried dissatisfactions in relationships that need to be released. You may feel the urge to firmly stand your ground, but it would be more beneficial to listen to what your family members have to say. They may offer you useful advice if you care to listen patiently with an open mind.

Managing interpersonal relationships will be your central theme this year, as how well you handle these challenges will greatly affect all the other areas of your life. The Grand Duke (太歲) and Earth Killing (地煞) are both Stars that denote possibilities of disruptions to the plans you make this year, especially when other people are involved. Stay level-headed at all times and watch your words and actions to ensure you will not be made a scapegoat for others.

The Earth Killing Star indicates disruptions to your plans, in particular delays in work-related projects. Delays and troubles surrounding your work projects this year are most likely the result of poor planning. Hence, it is advisable to always have a detailed plan at hand to follow closely. Do not wait until the last minute to start or finalise a project. Gather your information and resources well ahead of time so that you are able to cope with any ad-hoc changes at work.

This year, it is also important to take care of your mental and physical well-being. The presence of the Blood Knife Star (血刃), Instability Star (浮沉) and Sword Edge Star (劍鋒) signify heightened risks for injuries, accidents and health issues related to stress. Allow your body and mind to get enough rest to avoid burning out. Problems may seem overwhelming at first, but you can try breaking down big tasks into smaller, more manageable ones and tackling them one by one. It is also essential to refrain from driving or participating in extreme sports while in a state of fatigue. Ensure that you always get adequate rest time to boost your energy levels.

Life is what you make of it. Remember that what ultimately matters ultimately is how you deal with any given situation. With a positive never-say-die attitude, even though there will be obstacles in your way, you will be able to come out on top if you manage your plans well and stay on track. Maintain this mindset until the end of the year, and you will find yourself accomplishing far more than what you thought was possible!

The Forecast for Individual Aspects of the Year

 **Wealth**

There will be a slight lack of movement and development where money is concerned this year. However, this can be mitigated by curtailing overspending and high risk investments. Cushion that loss by purchasing something that will prove useful to you in order to keep that financial outward momentum to a minimum. Work hard, be proactive at work and endeavour to look for better savings plans with higher returns.

 **Career**

Prepare yourself for an eventful year in terms of career as you are bound to see a lot of movement where work is concerned. Try not to be your own obstacle this year in terms of career. Stay calm and modest while liaising with superiors and clients since a peaceful working environment will better your career prospects. Furthermore, the presence of the noblemen will provide you with help and aid when you need them. Should Pig individuals strive harder and work persistently, you shall be blessed with fine gain in your career.

 **Relationships**

In 2019, those who are single will have a lonely year ahead since their social lives will be rather dull and uneventful. However, single Pigs should not feel downtrodden with this development. Instead, shift your focus to other areas of life and practice patience for now as there will be certain months where Peach Blossom Luck will be in your favour. Pigs who are already in a committed relationship will enjoy a blissful and stable year.

Health

A not-so-good year of health is in store for Pigs this year as they will be prone to accidents. Nonetheless, you must treat this as a gentle reminder to be extra cautious in going about your daily life and being fully aware and attentive while driving on the road to avoid any accidents. Take extra care of your well-being to prevent unnecessary injuries. This year is also not the year to sign up for that parasailing adventure or scuba diving course, as there will be a likelihood of unavoidable mishaps.

Monthly Luck

農曆正月 (February 4th - March 5th) 丙寅

This will be a great month for you. However, bear in mind that there will be gossips and rumours that will dampen your mood in this month. To counter this, stand firm on your ground and do not let these petty riffs affect you. Keep your emotions in check and handle issues diplomatically. With this cheerful disposition you will be able to counter whatever the month brings your way.

農曆二月 (March 6th - April 4th) 丁卯

Similar to the previous month, Pig individuals will experience good career luck this month as well. Enhanced relationships with colleagues will allow them to start paying you more attention, which will subsequently give them the chance to appreciate the efforts that you pitch in as a team. Your focus on health matters must also remain your steadfast priority this month. Eat well and rest well. With your continuous effort to boost your well-being you will see better outcomes in terms of career development this month.

農曆三月 (April 5th - May 5th) 戊辰

Minor financial loss is in store for you this month, though it would not be anything detrimental. You are advised to purchase things that you love or to donate your money to a good cause as gesture of good tidings and as a symbolism to deter more financial loss.

農曆四月 (May 6th - June 5th) 己巳

Your quote of the month will be "No pain, no gain". Work this month might seem to bog you down and leave you in the dumps some days. There are always two sides to a coin and thus, treat this as opportunity to showcase your talent and capabilities at work. Also, work smart and stay proactive while rising up to meet tough challenges. With the persistence and perseverance, your superiors and colleagues will acknowledge your contribution to the team.

農曆五月 (June 6th - July 6th) 庚午

Blessed with the presence of the Nobleman Star, Pig individuals see ease while undertaking their tasks. As a result, you will be blessed with more time and focus in other equally important area of your life such as health. In that element, you should refrain from signing yourself up for any dangerous activities or sports, to avoid any potential accidents. Choose instead, to go for a light jog, a brisk walk or perhaps join a yoga class.

農曆六月 (July 7th - August 7th) 辛未

All is well for you this month, and henceforth you will find yourself executing plans with great ease and dexterity. As a reward for all your endeavours, your fortune in career, wealth and relationship will see positive outcomes this month. This change of tidings will fruit positive effects into your life, so be ready to embrace them and bask in the fruits of your labour!

農曆七月 (August 8th - September 7th) 壬申

This month you will enjoy lesser fortune when compared to the previous months abundance. Therefore, brace yourself for some strong tides and waves ahead. This is not a month to decide on undertaking adventures in extreme sports. Nevertheless, conform to the existing rules while dealing with matters in relation to work and stay grounded. By building a strong base you will reap steady development.

農曆八月 (September 8th - October 7th) 癸酉

This month will test your patience and the ability to work under pressure. It is always best to keep your expectations low to help ease the stresses from dealing with too many things. Though you might not be able to find as many solutions to problems, the help you receive will minimise you from being stretched too thin, and guide you throughout this month. Remember, "No pressure, no diamond", showcase your creativity in countering the elements. Perseverance and hard work will aid you in leaping over your hurdles.

豬

The Pig in 2019

農曆九月 (October 8th - November 7th) 甲戌

As the saying goes, "Speak when you are angry and regret the outcome", thus gossips and rumours are things that you must be wary of this month. Stay cool-headed and kind at all times, do not confront issues without having given it a thought or two or there could be dire consequences and some heated exchange.

農曆十月 (November 8th - December 6th) 乙亥

You will come across some speed bumps and unexpected hurdles this month. However, these are nothing but gentle reminders to reflect on your fast-pace style of working. Think before you act and slow down to avoid any negative repercussions. With the help of the somewhat decent fortune this month, coupled with your own effort, these issues will subside eventually.

農曆十一月 (December 7th 2019 - January 5th 2020) 丙子

Minor rumours and gossips and perhaps even monetary loss is in sight, so patience and endurance will be the keys for you this month! Try to be contented with the time you are blessed to spend with family members, rather than getting into unnecessary arguments with them. Remind yourself from time to time that tolerance is crucial for a peaceful household and family life.

農曆十二月 (January 6th - February 3rd 2020) 丁丑

Refrain yourself from deciding to invest in anything this month. Also watch what you say and perhaps keep that anger in check for a bit as a wrong word out of your mouth, would put a shoe in it, in its place. This inadvertently could lead to arguments. The best way to deal with petty individuals looking for a fight is to ignore them entirely. As the saying goes - "empty tins makes the loudest noise". All the negativities will ease as the days pass.

Rat 子

Year of the Rat

| 1924 | 1936 | 1948 | 1960 | 1972 | 1984 | 1996 | 2008 |

A person's Chinese age is obtained by adding one year to their Western birthday. For example, if you were born in 1976, your Western age in 2019 is 43, but your Chinese age would be 44.

Overall Forecast For The Year

 If you have any ambition to climb up the career ladder, this year is the perfect time to make your move as there are two auspicious Stars coming to your aid to boost your work performance and showcase your capabilities, so that you will shine in your workplace. As long as you have the skills and are prepared to put in the required effort, you will most likely soar in your career during the Year of the Pig, with an abundant of opportunities opening up for you.

Two extremely beneficial Stars will be on your side this year – the Sun Star (太陽) and the Heavenly Yi Star (天乙). While the Sun Star brings you ample opportunities to earn more profits and make breakthroughs in your career, the Heavenly Yi Star adds the cherry on top by sending you secret assistance through the Noble People in your life. The presence of both these auspicious Stars aligning together will help open new doors for you in career and business. You will find your social network expanding rapidly this year, which will bring you great opportunities to make financial gains.

The Sun is a highly optimistic Star, so it would be wise for you to make full use of the positive energy coming from the Sun Star this year by being proactive and executing your career goals and business plans. Find out what and who can bring you one step closer towards your dreams and make that first move boldly – be it sending out your resume for that dream job or finding investors for your new business venture. Do your groundwork well and you will most likely succeed in any career endeavours.

If you have been feeling like you are fighting all the battles alone at work, this year you will find kind people coming to help you out when in need, allowing you the time and space to take a breather once in a while as they have your back. Furthermore, there is likely assistance coming from behind-the-scenes that will give you just the right boost or lift you need to perform your best and stand out at your workplace, as you have the support of the Heavenly Yi Star this year.

While you savour the sweet taste of success, be mindful to remain humble and respectful when communicating with others, no matter what their positions are. This is because if you are not careful with how you carry yourself, you may run into troubles such as disputes and slander this year, as indicated by the presence of the Annual Sha Star (年煞). Remember to show your gratitude to those who have supported you all along, and pass the kindness on to others who in turn need your guidance and help.

As you focus on expanding your social network and growing your career this year, try not to neglect your loved ones or else your personal life might become a little barren. As shown by the presence of the Sky Emptiness Star (天空), even though you will meet and talk with many people who can open new doors in career and business, you may still feel lonely amidst all the social events you find yourself attending. It will do you well to go on a social or spiritual retreat once in a while to reconnect with yourself, or spend some quality time with loved ones to attain that important work-life balance.

Your increased popularity this year will also bring along temptations and dalliances that have the potential to damage your relationships and reputation. Therefore, it is best to avoid advances from others if you are married or already in a committed relationship. The presence of both the Salty Pool Star (咸池) and the Annual Sha Star indicate the possibilities of having problematic relationships this year, most probably due to a third party in the relationship. It is important to keep your promises and be faithful to your significant other. Treading on dangerous waters may cost you more than you would have imagined.

The Year of the Pig will bring new heights for you in career and business. Luck is what happens when preparation meets opportunity; now that you are equipped with the right capabilities, new doors will open in the new year with Noble People around to give you a push along the way. This year you will be rewarded for all the hard work and effort you have put forth in the previous years. As you celebrate your success, don't forget to share it with those supporting you!

The Forecast for Individual Aspects of the Year

 **Wealth**

The Rat's wealth path is probably not as smooth as its career outlook, however, there will be pockets of opportunities to capitalise on if you remain alert and open to new experiences. However, you need not be overly concerned as there will be aid to buffer and keep that financial loss to a minimum. This year will not bode well for any forms of speculative investment, gambling or loan taking.

 **Career**

The Rat's career forecast this year depends a lot on its ability to make the best opportunities; even if those opportunities appear slim at the beginning. With the right actions, mediocre results can become good, or good results can become great. Patience and perseverance are your two best friends this year in work. Some days will be challenging, but if you choose to embrace it rather than run away from it, you will definitely see the rainbow at the end of the cloud. On the other hand, being lazy or unconcerned with your work will only increase its complexity.

Relationships

If you are single, 2019 is not really a year to boost your love prospects. The year predicts that you might encounter difficulties in finding a partner. Married Rats need to be careful of the Salty Pool Star. Don't give in to external temptations – even what seem like mild flirtations – as it'll only lead to distress and trouble. Try to not agitate an already volatile situation and perhaps stop short from making wild comments and accusations.

Health

There might be a slight threat to your health this year – particularly from external factors. It is prudent to take care of your physical well-being and adopt a healthier lifestyle. Pay attention to food as the proper dietary intake will help in your overall well-being. Moreover, to counter the prospect of contracting epidemic diseases, make a habit to wear masks and carry disinfectants with you in case there is a need.

 **Monthly Luck**

農曆正月 (February 4th - March 5th) 丙寅

You are advised to avoid travelling this month, as you may encounter some issues of great inconvenience such as passport problems, long layovers and flight delays. In addition to that, you will encounter difficulties in your communication with others even with the simplest of conversations. Thus, it is crucial to think before you speak.

農曆二月 (March 6th - April 4th) 丁卯

This is a month where you have to exercise caution in everything you do. Things may not be smooth sailing in this period, as there is likelihood of you offending people in your social circle. This would result in rumours and gossips heading your way. To avoid any misunderstanding, you should pay wise attention to details and choice of words while communicating with friends and family. At the same time, it is best if you can refrain yourself from engaging in any high risk activities, ensuring your safety from body injuries.

農曆三月 (April 5th - May 5th) 戊辰

A huge change of fortune is in store for you, in fact you will enjoy excellent luck this month. It will allow you to execute plans freely and you will have ease in everything you do, fruiting positive and favourable results. You will find yourself being passionate for just about everything, resulting in an outstanding performance at work, thus earning precious compliments and trust from your superiors as a result. So stay cheerful and contented. Be grateful for the things around you.

農曆四月 (May 6th - June 5th) 己巳

Your good luck from last month will follow you through this month. Kind and friendly people who are likely to aid you in many areas in this month will surround you. In other words, you will have assistance if you are faced with difficulties. Should you have a keen interest in buying luxury goods namely properties, jewelleries, or some form of luxuries; you are likely to get them at a better deal this month.

農曆五月 (June 6th - July 6th) 庚午

"Go small, avoid big things" is the key for this month! If you have big plans brewing this month, practice your patience and carry those plans forward as you will probably face light obstacles or possible failures in seeing the execution of those plans.

農曆六月 (July 7th - August 7th) 辛未

Time and budget will not be on your side this month, thus it is looking to being a rather forlorn month. You will encounter some drawbacks particularly when you come across work with tight deadlines and budgets. Therefore, you are advised to place more effort and focus on these deadlines leaving ample room to deal with uncertainties.

農曆七月 (August 8th - September 7th) 壬申

Overall, this is nothing but a great month for you. Everything you need will be in sight, as you will be able to produce work with exceptional results. Stay grateful for everything you do, execute your plans with confidence, and the rest will take care of itself.

農曆八月 (September 8th - October 7th) 癸酉

The mighty Peace Blossom Luck is in sight again and hooray for love! Single Rats are advised to use this month to scout for potential love mates. He or she could be right around the block or possibly even under your very nose. Head out and head into a singles event, or a meet up session in your local area that will expand your social circle and put you on the right path to meeting the one!

農曆九月 **(October 8th - November 7th)** 甲戌
This month might see you confront some issues on things that you do. However, do not be fret, as the saying goes, "This too shall come to pass". Remind yourself to stay positive at all times, and help will arrive in the moments that you need them to.

農曆十月 **(November 8th - December 6th)** 乙亥
Obstacles in life are meant to be stepping-stones for you to grow and better develop your character. Therefore, do not allow issues at hand to disturb you but instead channel them for better character building.

農曆十一月 **(December 7th 2019 - January 5th 2020)** 丙子
There will be gossips and rumours about you this month that would need you to be extra watchful for. To counter this, stand firm on your ground and do not let these petty riffs affect you. Watch what you say and avoid conversations that carry an element of sensationalism and this may be your undoing.

農曆十二月 **(January 6th - February 3rd 2020)** 丁丑
A reversal of fortune from last month, you will be experiencing tremendous luck this month. The roller-coaster ride has reached its station and you can finally let that sigh of relief go. Like a calm after the storm. Unlike the previous months, things will move closer to your favour. So, get back on that horse and ride along to finish line.

Ox 丑

Year of the Ox							
1925	1937	1949	1961	1973	1985	1997	2009

A person's Chinese age is obtained by adding one year to their Western birthday. For example, if you were born in 1976, your Western age in 2019 is 43, but your Chinese age would be 44.

Overall Forecast For The Year

The year 2019 will offer you chances to look inward and focus on your internal happiness if you have not been spending much time taking care of your mental and emotional well-being. Trying to survive in the rat race may leave you with little time to look within as you continue to pursue external gratifications. Many external problems can be resolved if you first sort yourself out internally; this year will nudge you to get back on the right track.

A restructuring of your personal financial management may be necessary as you begin the year, because the presence of the Leopard Tail Star (豹尾) and the Great Sha Star (大煞) this year denote an increased risk of financial loss due to overspending, carelessness or recklessness. There may be a need to change your approach towards how you spend your money – ask yourself if you are buying certain things because you really need these things or because owning them would boost your image or make you feel good. Remember that material pursuits will only bring you temporary satisfaction; change your focus to look inward and you may find the root cause of this tendency to overspend.

If you have difficulties keeping track of your expenses, it may be handy to install personal finance management apps to help you record your income and expenses. This way, you can have a clearer overview of what you spend on and adjust your spending patterns to achieve your saving goals. For those who are planning to make investments in the new year, it will be prudent to do your research and get professional advice from analysts before taking the plunge. The presence of the Great Sha Star signifies recklessness and the propensity to make an unwise move in a hurry. Do not get pressured into making hasty decisions; make sure you take the time to consider all factors carefully before putting your money into an investment.

Likewise, be mindful when handling your valuables, as there is a heightened risk of losing valuables due to careless disposition. Check your seat before leaving the taxi or cinema, remember to take your wallet with you after paying your bill at the counter, and always make sure your valuables are with you at all times when outside. Make it a habit of putting all your items back into their proper place after use, so that you won't be rummaging through your house or bag when searching for certain items. Getting a bag with multiple compartments can also help you get better organized.

By putting your attention back on yourself and those close with you, you will also be able to build stronger bonds with your family this year. Spending more time with your family will enable you to detect any signs of illness, especially in elderly relatives. Paying more attention to their health and well-being is important this year due to the presence of the Funeral Door Star (喪門) and the Earth Funeral Star (地喪). The two Stars show the possibilities of declining health among the elderly members of your family. If any elderly member has a health condition, it is advisable to bring them for checkups regularly. It is also best to make sure they are always accompanied by someone, so that if they feel unwell there will be someone to call for help.

Besides taking care of your family members' health, you should also take care of your own well-being and be careful not to injure yourself due to recklessness, as the presence of the Flying Chaste Star (飛廉) this year could make you accident-prone. If you are working in a hazardous environment, be sure to adhere to all safety precautions; do not perform potentially dangerous tasks in a state of tiredness or sleepiness. Similarly, you should be mindful not to drive while feeling tired or unwell to avoid getting into accidents while on the road.

The Year of Pig will open up new opportunities for you to realign your life priorities if you have been neglecting your well-being and also your loved ones. It is tempting to keep chasing after money and fame, but remember that these things are all temporary; your mind and body will remain with you for a lifetime, so it's worthwhile to take good care of yourself. It is also essential to pay more attention to your family – after all, they are the ones who genuinely care about us.

The Forecast for Individual Aspects of the Year

 **Wealth**

2019 is a year where you should not be placing too much hope and expectations on personal wealth. That said, putting too much effort and focus onto one thing is never a good practice. Therefore, it would be wise to emphasize on balancing your financial input and output. Although monetary loss is unavoidable, it would not be detrimental for you to purchase things that you love or to donate your money to a good cause as a gesture of good tidings.

 **Career**

Your work life might see a slow decline which could see an additional few humps and bumps as things progress. This, in turn, would need some extra effort in putting things back on the right course. Nevertheless, an Ox is known as a tough, persistent and patient animal, thus the best solution to this temporary hurdle would be take some precautions, avoid risks and refrain from making extravagant purchases. It is wise to give your loyalty to your superior and heed their advice and directives. This in turn would build a great future foundation for yourself at work.

 **Relationships**

Whether you are single or in a relationship, 2019 is not really a year to boost your love prospects. The year is void of Peach Blossom Luck and as such you might encounter difficulties in finding a partner. For those already in a relationship, the year might bring some additional challenges that the two of you might need to work on. Exercise tolerance and understanding in dealing with these trials. Refrain from verbal arguments that may harm your relationship.

 **Health**

In 2019, emphasis should be placed on improving your health. Extra caution should be taken while crossing the road and driving to avoid accidents. In addition, as Ox individuals are vulnerable to illnesses and viruses, you should consult a doctor as soon as you feel unwell. Exercising more in your spare time would also help boost your health as a whole.

Monthly Luck

農曆正月 (February 4th - March 5th) 丙寅

This is a month where you will see an equal share of good and bad days. But, if Ox individuals to know their place, arm themselves with knowledge and respect people around them including themselves, they will have a pleasant and stable month eventually.

農曆二月 (March 6th - April 4th) 丁卯

This would be a tiring month for you, where you might feel exhausted from dealing with different matters or solving various issues. Unfortunately, even if you are weary, help and aid may not be readily available. Therefore, it is best to trust your own efforts, showcase your abilities and persevere as much as you can, and you will survive the month!

農曆三月 (April 5th - May 5th) 戊辰

Ox individuals should make it a habit to be cautious at all times, and refrain from extreme or dangerous activities, as they might injure or harm themselves in the process. Besides, you are advised to not lend money as there is a possibility that you might never see it again.

農曆四月 (May 6th - June 5th) 己巳

A huge change of fortune is in store for you, in fact you will enjoy excellent luck this month. It will allow you to execute plans freely and you will have ease in everything you do, fruiting positive and favourable results. So stay cheerful and contented and appreciate and be grateful for the things around you.

農曆五月 (June 6th - July 6th) 庚午

You are advised to be extra caution with people and things around you. The opposite sex, in particular, will probably affect you, causing unnecessary loss. But worry not, as you can be more attentive while expanding your network, avoid doing things out of the norm when trying to nurture relationships. While carrying out plans and work, it is best not to push yourself too hard, be natural and focus only on fulfilling your responsibility.

農曆六月 (July 7th - August 7th) 辛未

You might be facing one hurdle after another this month in things that you do. This might delay the progress of your plans and its outcomes. Therefore, focus is more well placed on building your personal value and being true to your responsibility, which would smoothen your fortune this month.

農曆七月 (August 8th - September 7th) 壬申

Strong fortune is in sight for you! Be prepared to have wonderful surprises happen around you, enjoy them as they are, and appreciate your life. Moreover, there is a strong chance to increase your income and finances, therefore this will be a great month for you in a whole.

農曆八月 (September 8th - October 7th) 癸酉

Carrying on from your good fortunes last month, you shall embrace even better fortunes this month. Be confident and dauntless while in your daily undertakings as you will find inordinate success in your endeavours.

農曆九月 (October 8th - November 7th) 甲戌

This month sees a slight reverse of your good tidings from last month. There might be some issues with relationships that will need your due attention. It would be wise to keep in check your choice of words you use during conversations. Be attentive to the attitude you use while communicating with others. Being humble and polite are two great characteristics to have in life. You may also try forgiving people for making mistakes with an open heart.

農曆十月 (November 8th - December 6th) 乙亥

This can be a really busy month, however, you should not neglect your own health while throwing yourself around to get things done. As the sayings goes, "health is your best wealth", you are advised to partake in self-care and task yourself accordingly. Maintaining a healthy body is the best way to ensure that you have the energy to look into tasks at hand.

農曆十一月 (December 7th 2019 - January 5th 2020) 丙子

After a month of endurance and patience, your fortune this month will see marked improvement, particularly in the areas of career and wealth. Should you have meetings and presentations that need your best performance, free yourself and be courageous enough to give it your best, as they will garner positive fruition.

農曆十二月 (January 6th - February 3rd 2020) 丁丑

Being more alert is the most pertinent advice for this month, as there might be unexpected misfortune heading your way. Although little monetary loss is unavoidable, it might be wise for you to purchase things you want or donate your money for a good cause.

Tiger 寅

虎

The Tiger in 2019

Year of the Tiger							
1926	1938	1950	1962	1974	1986	1998	2010

A person's Chinese age is obtained by adding one year to their Western birthday. For example, if you were born in 1976, your Western age in 2019 is 43, but your Chinese age would be 44.

Overall Forecast For The Year

All eyes will be on you as you take the center stage this year with the blessings of three very auspicious Stars, giving you the edge to truly shine and attract the attention of those who matter. With the aid of these fortunate Stars, you will certainly not want to waste the amazing opportunities that come your way by taking the back seat. It's high time you take the wheel and showcase your talents, as you will not be able to stay unnoticed for much longer this year!

If you have been working steadfastly in your career, take heart that your efforts will not go unnoticed much longer, for the presence of the National Treasure Star (國印) will boost your chances of getting deserved recognition for your work. In the Year of the Pig, all your hard work will bear fruit easily and you will be handsomely rewarded for your efforts with either a pay raise or a job promotion. With the blessings of the National Treasure Star, you will also find yourself gaining significant power and authority at your workplace. So, if you are seeking for career advancement, this is absolutely the year to ramp up your efforts for maximum results.

To further add to your good luck at work this year, the Grand Duke Combination Star (歲合) brings Noble People and mentors to assist you in times of need. These people may be your superiors, colleagues or friends who can offer you guidance and support. Additionally, with the presence of the Moon Star (太陰) this year, you can also count on receiving love and support from the female figures in your life.

As the Moon Star also enhances your ability to accrue wealth, this year will be a good time to make some long-term investments such as buying properties. Look out for valuable tips and recommendations from people around you; you may find good properties worth investing in. If you are a business owner, it will also be advantageous for you to invest in innovative technologies this year that could amplify your business profits. The opportunities to increase wealth will come in various ways; you just need to be quick enough to identify and grasp one.

With most of the spotlight on you, whatever you do or say will naturally come under close scrutiny. A casual slip of the tongue may result in bad blood with others. Therefore, it is vital to be tactful with your words and actions at all times. Form the habit of thinking before you speak this year, as three troublesome Stars related to arguments will increase the possibilities of you getting tangled up in conflicts, from petty gossip at best to litigation at worst.

The Heavenly Officer Charm Star (天官符), Piercing Rope Star (貫索) and Death God Star (亡神) denote the tendency to offend others unintentionally. Even if the miscommunication seems trivial, it has the likelihood to escalate into a serious issue this year. So, it is advisable that you hold your tongue when it comes to matters involving another's personal life or matters affecting another's reputation. Moreover, you should also control your temper to avoid heated arguments.

Keeping a clear mind is critical this year. Not only will you need clarity to perform and watch your steps, you also need it to stay determined on your goals. This year, the presence of the Hook Spirit Star (勾神) may cause you to feel confused and uncertain; when combined with the Solitary Star (孤辰) which causes a sense of loneliness, you may be easily distracted from what you originally set out to do. This may be the major obstacle this year for you to attain your goals. Stay focused and remind yourself of the reasons you set out to do something from time to time.

Overall, the Year of the Pig will be a rewarding one, as you will be given center stage to perform what you are capable of and the efforts you put in will pay off in the form of a pay raise or job promotion. What's more, you will be able to increase your wealth if you seize the opportunities when they arise. To reap all the rewards in the new year, make the effort to keep your mind clear, be aware of the consequences of your words and actions, and learn to differentiate whims from goals so that you do not easily deviate from your plans.

The Forecast for Individual Aspects of the Year

 **Wealth**

In 2019, you could do well to put more effort in being attentive in your communication with others. Watch what you say and choose to disclose to others. This may help you overcome gossips and rumours regarding financial issues. Furthermore, an important advice for you this year is to refrain yourself from being anyone's guarantor as there could be some formidable consequences to this decision. By practicing all the above, you shall experience a fair financial year, building up your income and savings as you go.

 **Career**

2019 brings the opportunity to exercise your tolerance with your superiors and colleagues. Everyone is unique in their opinions and therefore there might be times where these differing opinions might be tested and that is fine, as we should embrace difference. This would in turn, create a better and pleasant working atmosphere, which would enhance your own performance at work. In addition, if you were to cooperate well with your colleagues, a possible huge career advancement is on the horizon.

 **Relationships**

Even without Peach Blossom Luck, you are surrounded by great luck in relationship matters this year. Couples who are deeply in love may consider tying the knot. While single Tigers need not be upset, as you still stand a chance to meet your Mr. or Mrs. Right. Be aware of your surroundings and spend more time in getting to know your potential partner. Be brave in going for what you want.

 Health

You will enjoy good health this year. Having said that, you should still take great care to maintain that good health, by eating right and on time, and exercising.

Monthly Luck

農曆正月 (February 4th - March 5th) 丙寅

Fortune for this month is fair, though you might probably feel a little restless. You might be plagued with the thinking that you do not have the ability you may need to attain your goals, but if you are able to focus on fulfilling your responsibilities, the rest will take care of themselves. Also, it would be a good idea to watch what you say to others this month.

農曆二月 (March 6th - April 4th) 丁卯

Peach Blossom Luck is in your corner this month, Tigers and Tigresses! Unmarried men and women should pay attention to who is around you, and who knows your Mr. or Mrs. Right might be just around the corner. You will likely receive help and assistance from colleagues of the opposite sex in your quest for love but avoid allowing them to get too involved or things might get a little messy.

農曆三月 (April 5th - May 5th) 戊辰

This month will see you spend a little less time with your family members, therefore appreciate the time that you do get to spend with them and use it wisely. Communicate with them, listen to their needs, bridge better understanding as these would also likely hinder any possible misunderstanding and arguments.

農曆四月 (May 6th - June 5th) 己巳

You might encounter some hurdles that would curtail your performance at work this month; hence, you might feel more tired than usual due to your excessive workload. Again, just like the previous month, you might see lesser time spent with your family members. As you might probably feel slightly lonely this month, it would be a good time to reassert your independence and get to know yourself better with some quality "me time".

農曆五月 (June 6th - July 6th) 庚午

Patience is a virtue, Tiger. After two months of mixed fortune, your luck in this month will finally take turn for the better. Your reputation amongst your peers and colleagues will likely swell and this in turn will propel you forward with everything you do. Besides being fortunate in your career, your wealth too will see a better outcome this month.

農曆六月 (July 7th - August 7th) 辛未

This is a month where emphasis and care should be placed on your health so stand up and start exercising more! Go for a walk in the park, pick up a new sport with the family or some friends or start looking at some gym memberships. In addition, you might face some setbacks in some things that you endeavour to do, but help and assistance will not be far thus you need not worry when these problems rear their heads.

農曆七月 (August 8th - September 7th) 壬申

This month might see a mix of good and bad days so prepare yourself well to deal with any uncertainties. You will see some form of spiritual protection this month and therefore this will be your ally in any possible eventuality.

農曆八月 (September 8th - October 7th) 癸酉

You will have reasonably good fortune this month with executing plans you have been meaning to undertake. In all likelihood, you will probably see most of them come to fruition. You should also perhaps set aside some time to improving your health and being more robust.

農曆九月 (October 8th - November 7th) 甲戌

There is the likelihood of great stars for you in terms of career and wealth, therefore now is the time to walk into that office and ask for that raise you have always wanted. It is also wise to be a little more attentive to your surroundings as criminals might lurk in the dark corners.

農曆十月 (November 8th - December 6th) 乙亥

Honing in your luck from the month before, you will enjoy greater fortune this month. A word of advice for Tigers - always stay cheerful and contented, as you will find that, through your jovial ways, you will observe ease and joy in whatever you do. You will see some assistance and aid from the people around you. Be alert with what you say, as gossips and rumours occur when we miscommunicate.

農曆十一月 (December 7th 2019 - January 5th 2020) 丙子

You need to exercise caution this month as there will be hurdles that need you to prove your worth. If there are any pending plans, practice patience and think long and hard before coming to a decision. It would be wise to execute arrangements when you are truly prepared or delay them to the next month where time and opportunity will be on your side.

農曆十二月 (January 6th - February 3rd 2020) 丁丑

Peace Blossom Luck is here for you again! If you are single, this will be an excellent month for you to meet your Mr. or Mrs. Right, hence be on guard with your surroundings, and you might just bump into your perfect partner. However, if you already have your eye on a special someone, this is the month to steer your courage and ask him or her out! On the health front - you could endeavour to do more exercise and eat well during this and the following months.

Rabbit 卯

Year of the Rabbit							
1927	1939	1951	1963	1975	1987	1999	2011

A person's Chinese age is obtained by adding one year to their Western birthday. For example, if you were born in 1976, your Western age in 2019 is 43, but your Chinese age would be 44.

Overall Forecast For The Year

 Get ready for a fantastic year ahead, as you almost have it all within your grasp! Your wealth, career and relationship aspects will receive a significant boost from three highly auspicious Stars in the Year of the Pig. The only catch is that you will need to be mindful not to cut corners by taking any risky actions and you will likely achieve your personal ambitions this year.

You can expect good opportunities for accumulating wealth to come knocking on your door, as you have the Golden Lock Star (金匱) on your side this year. The Golden Lock Star, as its name indicates, is a wealth Star that enhances one's financial gain. When it is present, your chances of earning more profits, receiving larger bonuses and getting a pay raise will be greatly boosted. Be prepared so that when such opportunity arises, you have the required skills to make the most out of it.

The good news doesn't stop here; you also have the blessings of the Three Stages Star (三台) this year, enabling you to perform your best at work, at the same time improving your chances for career advancement. Not only is this Star favourable for career growth, it is also beneficial for those who run their own businesses. The Three Stages Star helps you to gain a comprehensive understanding of the market which allows you to respond quickly, so that you may swiftly seize any opportunities in a market gap to expand your business and increase your business profits.

You can achieve more when you work as part of a team. This year, you also have the good luck of being surrounded by noble and capable people, as the General Star (將星) is present. If you need assistance, don't be shy to reach out to others as you will likely receive help from sincere individuals to complete your tasks smoothly. If you are building a team, you will attract talented people to join you; just ensure that you provide an encouraging work environment and harness your leadership skills to retain these capable people. Even if you are not in a managerial role, you will likely find opportunities to showcase and improve your leadership skills.

With bountiful rewards within reach, you may feel anxious and impatient, as indicated by the presence of the Five Ghost Star (五鬼). This Star shows that you need to keep your emotions in check in order to preserve your good luck this year. The opportunities that come up will be overwhelming and you may feel inclined to flee from these challenging situations, or you may feel tempted to make an unwise move to achieve your goals. Either way, you have to be aware of your emotions and how they affect you. Make rational decisions instead of emotional or hasty ones, so that you won't regret them later.

Acting recklessly without considering the consequences will likely cost you dearly this year, as the Officer Charm Star (官符), Flying Charm Star (飛符) and Year Charm Star (年符) that are present signify increased possibilities of legal entanglements. There may be temptations to make risky moves while you rush to attain your goals but remember that it is not worth it to cut corners. It's better to take the high road than to land in trouble by breaking laws and regulations. As long as you stay on the right path, you will reach your destination no matter how long it takes.

If you are not wary of these legal matters and choose to break the law, it may cost a fortune. The Year Charm Star also indicates a risk of bankruptcy, which is the likely outcome if you get entangled in a court case. Court cases usually drag on for years and the emotional stress accumulated will certainly take a toll on your health, besides burning a hole in your pocket. Therefore, play safe and be smart when it comes to matters that may potentially be illegal or violate others' rights.

With three Stars favourable to your wealth, career and relationship aspects present, you will be most formidable this year. Make sure you are prepared to grab these opportunities to advance in life, so that you don't miss out on all the good things the Year of the Pig offers. Therefore, firmly plant both your feet on the ground and refrain from taking risky shortcuts to get to your desired destination. This way, you can be certain in reaching any goals you have set your eyes on!

The Forecast for Individual Aspects of the Year

Wealth

The Golden Lock Star and the Three Stages Star indicate that you'll be able to enjoy good wealth. Your financial management skills will considerably improve and you should reap the benefits of that. Those who have their own business will be able to earn a bit of money. Before committing to anything serious, make sure you obtain enough advice from financial experts or family members to help you formulate a solid and feasible decision.

Career

The Rabbit should enjoy good developments in career. There are very strong chances that you may be seeing an upgraded office space in terms of promotion and a fatter wallet in terms of a salary increment! Opportunities will arise and you should be brave enough to grab them and make the most out of them. This, combined with hard work, should see the Rabbit shinning admirably where career is concerned.

 **Relationships**

If you are in a relationship, consider popping the question or tying the knot with your partner this year. With the help and aid from friends and family, this union will be blessed and the marriage will bear great rewards. Furthermore, if you are still single, fret not - go on dates to better your chances of meeting someone great!

Health

In 2019, your overall attention and focus should be on your health as there will be some stumbling blocks of illnesses and injuries, though there will be no serious or major ramifications to this. Pay great attention to issues with your stomach and waist area. Refrain yourself from engaging in extreme sports and cut down on your intake of heaty and oily food.

Monthly Luck

農曆正月 (February 4th - March 5th) 丙寅

This month brings great tidings your way. While you are advised to stay proactive and strive harder for greater achievement, you should not try to force anything to be done at your pace, instead things will better work in your favour with better planning and steadfast execution. Also, refrain yourself from playing detective and speculating issues, as it will probably cost you big money.

農曆二月 (March 6th - April 4th) 丁卯

Carrying the good fortune from previous month, most of your tasks will have great progress and you will see benefit in return. Nevertheless, just as last month, avoid from making any speculation or taking any unnecessary risk. Therefore, just be yourself and focus on being a better person. Avoid attempting side business in an attempt to attract more cash as this might go sideways.

農曆三月 (April 5th - May 5th) 戊辰

This month will take you on a fortune rollercoaster, and like a rollercoaster you will experience some ups and downs. Also, like being on a rollercoaster, this might cause you to feel a little out of control. To aid this period - be more detailed and attentive when dealing with your plans and day to day tasks. Perhaps this is not the month to start living in style as this might see your cash balance dwindle.

農曆四月 (May 6th - June 5th) 己巳

Your good luck will continue in this month and you will make a new breakthroughs at work under the help of colleagues or leaders and get recognized by your boss. Your luck for wealth will change greatly, so avoid risky investments as this might lead to unscrupulous cheating.

農曆五月 (June 6th - July 6th) 庚午

You will still experience both good and bad days this month, but a little transformation will take place that will shift your fortune tides. However, even when you are faced with sluggish progression with matter at hand, it will not give you too much of hard time when you keep your head grounded and focus on fulfilling your responsibility.

農曆六月 (July 7th - August 7th) 辛未

Your patience and endurance with the previous month's misfortunes has finally paid off! Lady luck is smiling again and she will continue to improve as help and aid that you require reach out to you. Therefore, stay cheerful in body and mind. There are some surprising moments waiting for you, so stay tuned.

農曆七月 (August 8th - September 7th) 壬申

Last month's luck will not carry forward to this month, therefore perseverance and strength will be your two best friends. While trying to find your footing, you should spare some time to pay attention to your health. Make a schedule and try to have a balanced meal at the appropriate time. Monetary loss this month again is inevitable. In this regard, any monetary loss you might experience takes effect to block other potential negative elements.

農曆八月 (September 8th - October 7th) 癸酉

The saying "think three times before you act" is your key this month. There might be elements that make you vulnerable on making mistakes, thus avoid being careless and insensitive. Also some great advice for this month is to sidestep gossips, rumours as this would better your overall wellbeing.

農曆九月 (October 8th - November 7th) 甲戌

The fortune stars are back this month! As things are not yet on solid ground, any major arrangements should be decided only after careful consideration. When things move persistently a little better, things will progress in the right way.

農曆十月 (November 8th - December 6th) 乙亥

You will be experiencing a mix of fortunes this month. In terms of career, should you be more responsible and attentive to details, a rather stable development will be in store for you. There will be temptations lurking around, therefore prevent yourself from being too greedy, and for men in particular, stay away from alcohol and the opposite sex, to have a better fortune this month.

農曆十一月 (December 7th 2019 - January 5th 2020) 丙子

Like in the previous months, attention to detail is still the key. Beware of creating unnecessary issues by way of carefully observing your words and movements. Besides, you might be prone to certain illnesses and diseases, thus you should take care of your health more. Be alert and stay away from any potential accident. Also, watch your words to prevent gossips and legal matters.

農曆十二月 (January 6th - February 3rd 2020) 丁丑

"After the storm comes the sun" is the best way to describe your fortune this month. After months of persevering, you will enjoy having everything back on the right track. Those issues that were plaguing you for months will find their solution. Therefore find the courage to not give up. Rabbits always strive to hop on through stumbling blocks and you have done it so far.

Dragon 辰

Year of the Dragon

1928	1940	1952	1964	1976	1988	2000	2012

A person's Chinese age is obtained by adding one year to their Western birthday. For example, if you were born in 1976, your Western age in 2019 is 43, but your Chinese age would be 44.

Overall Forecast For The Year

Your focus will be on relationships this year, as the Stars bringing positive influences into your relationship area will come together to assist you. If you have been looking for the right person, or if you are planning to tie the knot, this year has all the right Stars to manifest your wishes into reality. The key to make this the best year ever for you? Go out and socialise! Expand your social circle and you will likely find people who could help you advance in some way.

For single Dragon individuals, the presence of the Red Matchmaker Star (紅鸞) this year is an extremely favourable sign to find your Mr. or Mrs. Right, as it is a Star favouring romantic tidings. The Star adds that extra charm to how you interact with others, especially the person you are interested in. Make use of this enhanced confidence and let your natural charm work its magic. With the aid of this romantic Star, you can be more at ease when expressing yourself. This will be a great boost for those of you who easily get nervous in conversations.

For those who are not looking, the Year of the Pig also sees you benefiting from socialising. The Red Matchmaker Star not only favours romance, it also brings more positive social activities to you. Conversations tend to be filled with joy and laughter, which helps you to relax and de-stress. You may also receive invitations to attend celebrations and social gatherings that you should not miss out on. There will be many reasons to celebrate, so let yourself get immersed in these moments of pure bliss; you will find yourself feeling refreshed and rejuvenated afterwards.

Meeting new people isn't just about romance, of course. Another joyful Star at your side this year is the Monthly Virtue Star (月德), which brings new relationships that are helpful and supportive. As you expand your social circle this year, you are more likely to meet with like-minded people and people who could offer you valuable insights on career, business and wealth management.

Not only will you be able to make new friends with common interests, you will also find support and guidance from the people you meet. Therefore, it's time to become socially active if you have not been active before; go on a group hiking trip, attend your high school classmate's wedding dinner or make the effort to meet your friends over coffees and cakes during the weekend. The Stars can't help you if you don't take the first step!

While your social life will be filled with much positivity this year and you may get a little carried away by these jubilant social events, remember not to splurge too often and overspend. The Lesser Consumer Star (小耗) indicates the increased possibility of financial losses due to extravagant spending. It is advisable to keep track of your personal expenses, so that you are aware where your money goes to. Cut down on unnecessary spending or go for more affordable meals while eating out with friends. There are always cheaper alternatives; you don't have to stay at home and avoid social activities altogether in order to save more of your earnings.

Amidst all these happy occasions, you should also pay more attention to your elderly relatives especially the senior male family members. The presence of the Death Charm Star (死符) this year signifies the likelihood of a male elderly in the family in need of health support. Bring any elderly family member for medical checkups to detect early signs of health deterioration. Talk to them regularly to find out if there is anything amiss with their well-being. This is important so that you can get them the most effective treatment at the early stage of any illnesses.

To maximise the advantages you could gain from the Year of the Pig, Dragon individuals will need to take the first step to go out and meet people. Although you may feel like avoiding social events at times, it will do you well to come out of your shell and mingle with people this year. The Stars are aligned to bring you the best opportunities to make friends – and partners – for a lifetime, so you will stand to gain more than what you put in if you make the move to be socially active. Step outside and start creating moments to be cherished with the people you meet!

The Forecast for Individual Aspects of the Year

 **Wealth**

In 2019, you might need to watch out for gossips and rumours that come your way as this will affect your finances both directly and indirectly. Dragons are animals that symbolise great prosperity in ancient China, thus, this will equally be a good year in terms of financial wealth. However, be wary of pick pockets and thieves at all times. In order to not lose an inordinate amount of money, you will need to keep a close eye on your wallet. As an ambitious Dragon you may want to think about different forms of investment that could possibly add to your passive income.

 **Career**

Your career will be a non-issue this year and there will be no serious tides to haggle with. Relationships with your superiors will see better ascension this year, prompting for better career advancements and even a promotion. That said, being able to perform in your newly elected position greatly depends on your health and well-being. Therefore, avoid pushing yourself too hard and falling into the trap of illnesses.

 **Relationships**

If you are a single Dragon, love may come your way if you keep your eyes wide open. If you are looking to tie the knot, this would be the perfect year to do as the relationship will likely stand the test of time through the years. Married couples on the other hand will see their relationship flourish and get to enjoy growing together further as one unit.

 **Health**

This year might see you being more susceptible to illnesses and injuries, but they are of minor concern and nothing to be too worked up about. That said, there must be some concerted effort on your part to be more proactive in engaging in a better physical lifestyle and adopting a routine. A better body and mind will allow you to strive and push further in your other areas of life as well.

 Monthly Luck

農曆正月 (February 4th - March 5th) 丙寅

Persistence and hard work will be your two best allies this month. This month might see several stumbling blocks to hurdle through which will test your personal values. However, light shines brighter through dark skies and you will navigate through this rough waters with grace and great perseverance.

農曆二月 (March 6th - April 4th) 丁卯

"A healthy outside starts from the inside". Our bodies are a reflection of not only what we physically consume, but also what we put into our minds. Be mindful of your health particularly your digestive well-being. Avoid consuming raw food as it may contain viruses that might result in unnecessary health issues.

農曆三月 (April 5th - May 5th) 戊辰

This month will see you feeling a little more fatigued than usual, therefore take regular rest particularly when you feel weary and tired. Pay close attention to your finances and watch for gossip and rumours concerning you and the people around you. Whether you are at work or at school, be wary of the things you do, work hard to maintain your performance and progression.

農曆四月 (May 6th - June 5th) 己巳

A subtle change in fortune will propel you in most areas of your life. Use this upturn to make better choices and decisions. The rally of good fortune around you will be the subtle boost that you need to motivate you and discover new endeavours and solutions to issues that may have been plaguing you the month before.

農曆五月 (June 6th - July 6th) 庚午

The Chinese believe, "Minor illnesses is a form of blessing". Sometimes, we as human beings need friendly reminders from the Universe to keep our health in check and to look after ourselves a little more. There is no need to sound the alarm on this, as any health issue will be minor. Take time for yourself, rest when needed and stop once in a while to smell the roses.

農曆六月 (July 7th - August 7th) 辛未

Life is a cycle and therefore we never know which way the wheels will turn on most days. There will be days this month where you might be left confused and dumbfounded on the direction of a decision you must take. There will be guiding hands for your daily tasks. Remain courteous, be it at home or at work and abide by the rules. These virtues will carry you through the course of the month.

農曆七月 (August 8th - September 7th) 壬申

This month sees a favourable change of fortune from last month's inauspicious stars! You will enjoy better prospects in terms of wealth and career. If you have been contemplating a career change or some form of career development, this is the month to do so! Likewise, your popularity among peers and friends are also soaring. This month will see you become a regular socialite, so buy some nice clothes and clear your calendar! It might just help find that key ally in your career.

農曆八月 (September 8th - October 7th) 癸酉

This month signals another month of great prosperity. Career wise, you will enjoy great cooperation from superior, colleagues and clients, thus resulting in a fruitful endeavour in this front. Dragon students will likely receive better results at school provided that they work hard whereas single Dragons might be able to meet their potential partner if they are persistently looking.

農曆九月 (October 8th - November 7th) 甲戌

A piece of important advice this month would be to "refrain yourself from doing anything big". Big plans equals big risks which essentially means that things can either go north or south. It is best to stick to the basics this month, rather than try to become a mover and shaker of new ideas. There is a likelihood that trying to branch out into new territories may not yield positive results.

農曆十月 (November 8th - December 6th) 乙亥

Another month to let your inner socialite shine through. By placing yourself and mingling in the right social circle you let your own unique individual light shine through. Thus, aiding your career and attaching yourself to the right raft that will pull you into better shores which seems to be this month's highlight.

農曆十一月 (December 7th 2019 - January 5th 2020) 丙子

Exercise is an amazing way to keep healthy while maintaining and keeping track of that extra weight that could be building up from all those hours sitting in front of a computer. However, it would be wise to pace yourself this month as there could be a likelihood of some form of injury in relation to your overzealousness on the circuit training course.

農曆十二月 (January 6th - February 3rd 2020) 丁丑

This month will see the value of yin and yang as this will be mirrored in your stars as well. Much of the bad you experience this month will be caused by gossips and rumours perpetrated by those not in your favour. However, this is balanced out by the well intentioned individuals who will be in your court and will try and call things out when they are disproportioned. This balance allows you to sail through the month somewhat unscathed.

Snake 巳

Year of the Snake							
1929	1941	1953	1965	1977	1989	2001	2013

A person's Chinese age is obtained by adding one year to their Western birthday. For example, if you were born in 1976, your Western age in 2019 is 43, but your Chinese age would be 44.

Overall Forecast For The Year

Buckle up and settle in for a bumpy ride in 2019, as this year will be full of challenges and unexpected changes. These changes will likely manifest in both your personal and professional life, so you will need to maintain the right mindset in order to triumph over any obstacles you encounter. Perseverance and patience will be key for Snake individuals in the Year of the Pig. Also, you should pay special attention to the physical well-being of your loved ones.

You may start the year bursting with fresh new ideas and ambitious plans, but you could soon see your plans go awry with the combined presence of the Obstacle Star (闌干) and Month Emptiness Star (月空). The two stars indicate a steep uphill climb to attain your goals in the coming year, as a result of setting unrealistic goals or spreading yourself a little too thin. Do take the time to plan carefully before embarking on a new venture; instead of reaching for the stars, focus on managing and completing the current tasks at hand to the best of your ability.

The Obstacle Star, as its name indicates, will bring you some hurdles as you set about to put your plans into action. You may find yourself needing to work extra hard to accomplish your tasks or feeling as though you are not making much headway despite your best efforts, as a result of unforeseen circumstances this year. Do not lose heart; prepare for all possible situations and have contingency plans so that you can react well to setbacks as they happen. As the saying goes, it is not what happens to you that matters most, but how well you react to it.

Also having influence is the Month Emptiness Star which may compel you to pursue lofty goals and ambitions, which aren't always very realistic nor attainable. This is not to say that you do not have the potential to achieve great success. However, you might encounter more difficulties than usual this year; keeping your head in the clouds with unrealistic or impractical dreams could backfire and result in a financial loss if you are not careful. It is advisable that you review your goals for 2019 and honestly assess your current capabilities to avoid biting off more than you can chew. Expending much energy and time chasing after lofty goals may cause you to be unnecessarily stressed or demoralized. Plant your feet firmly on the ground, slow down and live fully in the present. Use your time to improve your skills and be prepared for 2019.

This coming year also indicates the tendency to spend money aimlessly, due to the effect of the Great Consumer Star (大耗). You may be tempted to make risky huge investments without doing due diligence or spend carelessly on luxurious goods to maintain a certain lifestyle. Perhaps you will feel like splurging on ornate decorations for your home or signing up for expensive gym memberships. These expenses may bring you pleasure, but they are short-lived. Cut down on extravagant spending and learn to start saving. You may want to get advice on how to start a sensible saving plan to give yourself more financial security for the future.

Look for the unexpected in the Year of the Pig, as there will be some unsettling changes as denoted by the Year Breaker Star (歲破). These changes can bring positive or negative outcomes. Allow yourself to go with the flow instead of swimming against the tide. You can make changes work in your favour by keeping an optimistic outlook. Do not fear change; it brings opportunities for growth and learning. It is only when you are shaken out of your comfort zone that you can find a truly fresh perspective.

Tying in with the Year Breaker Star is the Sky Horse Star (驛馬) which indicates extensive travelling for you in 2019. Even though your career may not advance as smoothly as you would like this year, there should be good opportunities for travel as a result of your job or to further your education. If you have the chance to travel, do it as you will find these trips to be personally enriching and beneficial in the long run.

As you meet the challenges that await you in 2019, it is also advisable to put aside enough time to spend with your family, due to the presence of the Pealing Head Star (披頭). This star increases the risk of ill health or death in the family or household. So, by paying extra attention to your family, you will be able to notice if anyone seems to be feeling unwell and take them for an early checkup. Spending quality time with your family will also strengthen your family bonds. Remember that even when everything seems to be going wrong, you will always have the comfort of your family to return home to.

The Forecast for Individual Aspects of the Year

 **Wealth**

2019 needs to see you strike a balance within your finances. There needs to be a good balance of money gained and money spent. This is essential so as to not lose any more money than what already seems to be a year of draining financials. Therefore, perhaps making that trip to the casinos this year may not be the best of ideas. When there is an element of financial loss, it is always good practice to cushion that loss with a symbolic 'loss' by purchasing something that will prove useful to you.

 **Career**

This year will see you being bogged down by stressful work constraints that you might take special heed to. With proper rest and family time you will certainly pull through the stresses of work. You might experience some form of face off with your bosses due to perhaps their inability to understand your current predicament. Exercise calm and patience when threading through these situations as they won't be for long and you will certainly be rewarded. Your strength and fortune still lies within the industry that you are in, thus thinking about updating your resume for a job shift is unwise.

 Relationships

This year proves to be a rather lack lustre year for Snake individuals due to the weak Peach Blossom star. If you are attached, refrain from engaging in any unwanted arguments and instead try and to foster a better relationship with deeper understanding. Plan a holiday or head out to that romantic restaurant you've been thinking of trying! As for the single Snakes, this year would be a great year to get to know yourself. Sometimes in order to become a better partner, one must first be in tune with oneself.

 **Health**

Generally, you should not have to be overly concerned about major health problems this year. You may have to endure minor ailments such as the occasional fever or cold. It is prudent to employ better driving etiquette to steer clear of possible accidents on the road. It would also be in your favour to be extra cautious when preparing your favourite family meal in the kitchen. Observe a healthy diet and exercise regularly to keep your health at an optimal level to battle the problems in other areas of your life.

 **Monthly Luck**

農曆正月 (February 4th - March 5th) 丙寅

This will be a great month for you. Do not allow yourself to be restricted and do not place restrictions on yourself. Enjoy the month and its blessed tidings. Take time to smell the roses and the coffee. Though there might be some bumps to drive over, you will receive the help you need from those around you.

農曆二月 (March 6th - April 4th) 丁卯

Work this month might seem to bog you down and leave you in the dumps some days. You might find that you will be asked to jump through hoops and dodge arrows being shot at you from different directions. However, best treat this as a learning curve and use this as an opportunity to showcase your skills and talents. When you are able to work hard and persistently, you will be rewarded and acknowledged by the others, fruiting positive results.

農曆三月 (April 5th - May 5th) 戊辰

A change of fortune is in store for you this month! You will see things in a new light this month and some things unknown to you might come as a pleasant surprise. On the other hand, as the saying goes "Too much of anything is never a good thing", you should also be aware of bad hats lurking around that may pose as a potential risk.

農曆四月 (May 6th - June 5th) 己巳

This is the month where it would be wise to put your observation skills to good use. Keep an eye out on things that might be of use to you and might also work to the opposite of your goals. Exercise wariness to things that may bring you harm. This month might also be a dud in your plans to having good quality family time and therefore, be grateful for whatever time you get to have with them.

農曆五月 (June 6th - July 6th) 庚午

You will see this month progressing a lot slower than the previous months. And sometimes slow is good as all good things take time to manifest. As the saying goes 'Rome wasn't built in a day'. Take your time in devising a good plan of outcome and be persistent in the changes you want to see in the relevant areas of your life. Channelling this persistency into other areas of your life such as wealth and health would also possibly do you a world of good.

農曆六月 (July 7th - August 7th) 辛未

Things may not all go smoothly this month, therefore brace yourself for some strong tides and waves ahead. You might be at loggerheads with certain people this month, particularly those in your work environment but remember to remain calm and channel good zen into yourself that will help give you the presence of mind in creating valuable outcomes for your situation.

農曆七月 (August 8th - September 7th) 壬申

The mighty Peach Blossom Luck is in sight again and hooray for love! Single Snakes are advised to use this month to scout for potential love mates. He or she could be right around the block or possibly even under your very nose. Sign up for a singles event, or a meet up session in your local area that will expand your social circle and put you on the right path to meeting the one!

農曆八月 (September 8th - October 7th) 癸酉

Your relationships with friends and colleagues will see its best light this month. It's time to pick up your phone and perhaps call that one friend that you have been meaning to reconnect with for ages but haven't got around to doing it. Or perhaps, take some time out and head on out to lunch with your colleagues and perhaps one of them might end up becoming your best friend.

農曆九月 (October 8th - November 7th) 甲戌

Some small monetary loss is unavoidable and therefore this is another month to perhaps cash that negative flow into some form of symbolic purchase for yourself. Besides buying these items will give you a better sense of self and also allow you to be grateful for what you have.

The Snake in 2019

農曆十月 (November 8th - December 6th) 乙亥

This month you will enjoy lesser fortune when compared to the previous months abundance. You might see your efforts and work ridiculed on some level and you might even find yourself not taken seriously in some tasks that you have put in charge with. Persevere on and you will find yourself out of the storm soon enough.

農曆十一月 (December 7th 2019 - January 5th 2020) 丙子

All is well for you this month, and henceforth you will find yourself executing plans with ease. This change of tidings will fruit positive effects into your life, so be ready to embrace them and bask in the fruits of your labour! Likewise, you will see a small rise in your bank account possibly from an unexpected income, but refrain yourself from making any major investment move at this particular time.

農曆十二月 (January 6th - February 3rd 2020) 丁丑

You will see a rather chunky change of luck this month. Having said that, be dauntless in executing your day to day activities and you will see that your ever endeavour will bring you that pot of gold you endeavour. Your relationship with family members will improve significantly this time around too due to the fact you have more time to spend with them.

Horse 午

Year of the Horse							
1930	1942	1954	1966	1978	1990	2002	2014

A person's Chinese age is obtained by adding one year to their Western birthday. For example, if you were born in 1976, your Western age in 2019 is 43, but your Chinese age would be 44.

Overall Forecast For The Year

2019 promises to be exciting and wonderful for you with the positive energies of auspicious Stars backing you up! Get ready to enjoy all the good fortune coming your way and bask in the generally happy atmosphere with a flourishing social life. Furthermore, you can look forward to increasing your wealth and having the support of generous people.

One of the biggest signs in your corner is the Dragon Virtue Star (龍德), which suggests an overall sense of positivity and good omens. You can expect to have a smooth-sailing year and lots of happy occasions with your loved ones. Lady luck is smiling down at you, so much so that you will find yourself having the Midas Touch when it comes to picking the right business or investments to accumulate your wealth. You will be able to successfully deal with any problems that arise in unexpected situations and turn the tables in your favour.

In the Year of the Pig, you can also expect to have flourishing relationships with the combined effect of the Emperor Star (紫微) and Earth Relief Star (地解). Both Stars denote Noble People coming to your aid in times of need. With the blessings of these Stars, you should have all the confidence to go forth and pursue your dreams as all signs are looking up for you.

The Emperor Star indicates that you can gain much happiness and contentment through strong relationships with others in the coming year. Noble People will offer you crucial guidance and assistance when you most need it. These individuals could be your friends and family, or random people who come along at the right time to provide you with useful support for all your endeavours. Additionally, you will find yourself surrounded by positive and kind people in your social circle or in your work place which makes your life so much more harmonious. If you are leading a team, you will receive positive synergy with people working to lift you higher.

Your good luck continues with the influence of the Earth Relief Star. This auspicious Star indicates that you will have an extra edge in problem-solving, especially when it involves other people. Doors will open for you more easily in 2019, as you will have the charm to get people to back you up in many situations. Therefore, it is the right time to be socially active as you'll be able to make new friends with people sharing common interests and similar values.

With all these favourable Stars sending you positive energy, you will be on top of your game and feeling unstoppable. However, you should pay heed to your safety as the Dark Sky Star (天厄) indicates that you will be prone to getting into minor accidents. Try to get enough rest so that you can stay alert when you are out and about. Do not drive when you are feeling tired; get a friend to send you home instead or take a cab. Be careful when using any sharp tools or electrical equipment. While the injuries you are likely to suffer will be minor, you can avoid accidents altogether by being more cautious and aware of your surroundings.

Aside from the Dark Sky Star, you should also be wary of the Brutal Defeat Star (暴敗) which brings the possibility of unexpected twists and turns in 2019. While your fortune will remain strong in the coming year, your wealth luck could be affected and plans may derail if you act recklessly or try to cut corners to achieve success. Keep a cool head and think things through. You will need to be quick to adapt and come up with alternative plans when unexpected changes occur.

Overall, you will have a lot of good news and joyous moments to look forward to in the Year of the Pig. With generous blessings from the Dragon Virtue Star, Emperor Star and Earth Relief Star, you could reach a new career breakthrough or make your long-held ambitions come true. This is the year to finally do what you have always dreamt of doing – be it changing your career, building that dream house or starting that floral business - as you will receive help and support from the people around you. Fortune favours the bold; make the first move in order for your lucky Stars to help you!

The Forecast for Individual Aspects of the Year

 **Wealth**

Your overall fortune in wealth for 2019 is excellent. Though a slight monetary loss is unavoidable. Perhaps, as a form of symbolic financial loss, spend your money on some form of assets or perhaps purchase something you may have had your eye on. As you will be gaining good profits from various quarters, be wise in handling these vast amounts of incoming cash and utilize them wisely. Also, with the help of this year's fortune, you will be blessed with more flexibility for better endeavours in the following financial year.

 Career

2019 will be a fine career year for you. Fortune will be further at your side post autumn season. This is the time to make improvements within yourself and perhaps update that resume for that position you have had your eye on for years. Horse individuals will always go all out in executing plans, gaining performance recognition in the process. Also, a timed execution of plans is essential in ensuring an organised outcome rather than a haphazard implementation of plans which would lead to confusion and chaos.

 **Relationships**

Peach Blossom Luck is in your corner this year! You are surrounded by great luck in relationship matters this year. Couples who are in a committed, loving relationship may consider tying the knot this year. Things will bode well for these love birds and a union will rise despite the tides and remain prosperous. Single mares and studs need not be upset, as you still stand a chance to meet your Mr. or Mrs. Right this year. Be aware of your surroundings and spend more time in getting to know your potential partner. Be brave in going for what you want and be bold on dates. Let your true self shine through.

 **Health**

Horses will be able to dodge injuries and illnesses this year. That said, focus on your diet and exercise plan, as a healthier body will motivate you to work even harder. As for senior Horses, place extra caution on your diet and food intake. Eat the right food at the right time and avoid skipping or having late meals. This might cause to have stomach-related issues and as the saying goes – "It's always better to be safe than sorry".

 Monthly Luck

農曆正月 (February 4th - March 5th) 丙寅

Though faced with issues and stumbling blocks this month, Horses will be blessed with having protection and assistance from family, colleagues and even your superiors. Despite the arrival of a testing month, aid will be with you when the need arises. Be patient and prepare yourself well for everything that is coming.

農曆二月 (March 6th - April 4th) 丁卯

This month will see a good balance of yin and yang. You will enjoy better prospects in terms of wealth and career. Embrace the good times when they stop by and enjoy the sun that shines through after the stormy skies. As for the single Horses, this month would be a great time to get to know people around you. If you have an eye on someone – ask them out! Be courageous and have faith that Cupid's arrow picks you.

農曆三月 (April 5th - May 5th) 戊辰

Things may not all go smoothly this month, therefore brace yourself for little tides and waves ahead. You might see your efforts at work or even at home going unappreciated and unnoticed. Take proper care of your finances and perhaps curtail overspending on your part. Remember to remain calm and channel good energy all around. This will help give you the presence of mind in creating valuable outcomes for your situation.

農曆四月 (May 6th - June 5th) 己巳

More attention and focus should be placed on your health this month. Moderacy is key as such Horses should watch what they eat, avoid excessive intake of unhealthy food and take time out of busy schedules to exercise regularly. It would be best to avoid extreme and dangerous activities this month as there is a likelihood of injuries resulting from it. A better body and mind will allow you to strive and push further in your other areas of life as well.

農曆五月 (June 6th - July 6th) 庚午

The stumbling blocks placed in your path this month are meant to be stepping stones to shape you into becoming a better person. Therefore, do not allow issues at hand to disturb you but instead channel them for better character building. It would be wise to watch what you say to others and think carefully of your intended meaning in any communication you undertake this month. This will greatly aid you in sidestepping rumours and gossips. There might also be some bad hats lurking in your path and therefore you are advised to stay alert at all times.

農曆六月 (July 7th - August 7th) 辛未

All is well for you this month with a fantastic change of fortune. You will see an ease in executing plans as the stumbling blocks and impediments of last month will be gone. Your relationship with colleagues will be further enriched in this period of time as you will find common ground that will bond you. Single Horses should pay attention to who is around you this month, as your Mr. or Mrs. Right might be just around the corner from where you are.

農曆七月 (August 8th - September 7th) 壬申

This will be a wise month to keep your finances in check and curtail overspending. Perhaps as a form of symbolic financial loss, spend your money on something you require need. This is also a good month to get as much rest and relaxation you can afford to get, as in all likelihood it will be a tiring month. In addition, you may come across an opportunity for an overseas travelling stint either for a holiday or even work.

農曆八月 (September 8th - October 7th) 癸酉

A minor change of fortune for Horse individuals this month. Single Horses will see an expansion of their social circle and possibly meeting their Mr. or Mrs. Right. Married couples should work to foster a closer bond with your spouse. This may help prevent any possible intrusion by an ill-intentioned third party.

農曆九月 (October 8th - November 7th) 甲戌

This month will test your strength, independence and courage, particularly in your ability in solving problems that may spring your way, singlehandedly. Do not be troubled by this and use this as an opportunity to showcase your skills and talents. As long as you focus on the problem objectively and concisely, the solution is not very far away.

農曆十月 (November 8th - December 6th) 乙亥

Your good fortune will see a continuation this month. Your work life will be a non-issue this month and there will be no serious tides to haggle with. Your relationship with your superiors will see better ascension as they will be more open to listening to your ideas and queries, prompting for better career advancements and even a prospects. This tide allows to sail through the month somewhat unscathed.

農曆十一月 (December 7th 2019 - January 5th 2020) 丙子

You will come across certain setbacks this month. Though it will be nothing to be overly concerned with. Though this month is littered with possible hurdles, being studly Horses, you will still be able to use your strong legs to leap over fences and barrel down the track with great force and vigour. Though, there will be some problems that may see an instant solution, Horse individuals will be able to at least minimise them.

農曆十二月 (January 6th - February 3rd 2020) 丁丑

This will be a pleasant month for you, a turn of tides from the previous months. Do not allow yourself to be to be too caught up on things and do not place restrictions on yourself. Enjoy the month and the blessings that come with it. Work hard and put your best foot forward to gain the attention of the people around you. You will receive the help you require from those around you, when you cross that bridge.

Goat 未

Year of the Goat							
1931	1943	1955	1967	1979	1991	2003	2015

A person's Chinese age is obtained by adding one year to their Western birthday. For example, if you were born in 1976, your Western age in 2019 is 43, but your Chinese age would be 44.

Overall Forecast For The Year

The previous year has most likely been a rather eventful one for you, leaving you feeling a little breathless. The Year of the Pig will arrive just in time to give you a welcomed respite. In 2019, you have the opportunity to take better care of yourself, review your goals, make changes to your lifestyle and recharge yourself. Be patient and learn to empathize with others to avoid any miscommunication in your dealings. Your well-being is another area you should pay attention to.

The Elegant Seal Star (華蓋) heralds an auspicious time for your career to flourish, especially if you are working in a creative field such as architecture, designing or publishing. With the positive energies flowing your way this year, you can bring your professional pursuits to new heights. Your creative efforts could earn the praise of your superior and put you in the spotlight, which will increase your confidence and independence. Perhaps you've always wanted to indulge in an artistic hobby like painting, pursue a new skill or work in the creative field. By all means, just go for it this year and you will feel an immense satisfaction by doing so.

However, if you do nothing with your talents and do not find an outlet for your creative juices, this Star will have some negative side effects in other areas of your life. In particular, it will show up in areas of communication and connection. Think of the eccentric artist who is hard to please and often misunderstood. When you don't fulfill that inner yearning of yours for creative pursuits, it could lead to frustrations which make you come off as being haughty or standoffish to the people around you. Therefore, it is best to channel your creative energy into your personal passion projects at work or during your leisure hours as they will most certainly bring you joy, if not rewards and recognition.

Working in tandem with the Elegant Seal Star is the Sky Warrior Star (天雄), which indicates serious communication difficulties in the year ahead if you allow your frustrations to get under your skin. You must not over-react or let your emotions get the better of you when faced with difficulties, as it could lead to people getting the wrong impression about you. A careless word uttered without thinking can be misinterpreted by others, and this could lead to a breakdown in the relationship.

As the Star of miscommunication is having its effect on you this year, it would be prudent to mind your words and take the time to communicate clearly what you mean, so as to prevent any misunderstandings that may disrupt your personal and professional relationships. When you feel upset or pressured, it is wise to write down your thoughts and give yourself time to cool down. You may also seek a trusted friend or confidant willing to listen to you vent about your frustrations and give you some advice.

Aside from that, play it safe by not taking part in any risky activities as the White Tiger (白虎) indicates the heightened possibility of accidents occurring this year. Ensure you take all safety precautions by checking that your car is in top condition before going on any long road trip; try to avoid driving when feeling fatigued. Follow instructions carefully before operating any dangerous equipment to avoid getting into accidents. Don't walk on wet patches on the pavement and always be aware of your surroundings when you are out. Now is not the best time to try out any extreme sports or activities that might be physically demanding.

Additionally, you may feel increased uneasiness and anxiety due to the influence of the Sky Cry Star (天哭). Your emotional and mental health is especially vulnerable this year, which makes you extra sensitive to the events going on around you, both good and bad. It is wise to protect yourself from getting unduly affected by other people's behavior or things happening outside of your control. Focus on your own goals and spend more time with the people who matter to you. There is no need to carry the weight of the world on your shoulders, for it is a burden too great to bear by one person. Do not be afraid to confide and share your burdens with people you trust and ask for their advice.

The Year of the Pig can be a fulfilling one for Goat individuals, if you take the opportunity to explore and nurture your creative talents, whether it be for work or pleasure. Find an outlet for creativity and you will shine brightly. You may have some communication issues and difficulty connecting to others, but these are minor problems that can be overcome with tact, empathy and awareness.

The Forecast for Individual Aspects of the Year

 **Wealth**

In 2019, you will experience a better year in terms of wealth. When stumbling blocks are placed in front of you with regards to finances, you will see people rally around you to help contribute solutions. Furthermore, you will get the opportunity for you to shine at work, and those who were naysayers will eventually acknowledge you and your efforts.

 **Career**

You are advised to watch your communication this year. This is to avoid any misunderstanding and arguments that may arise. In case of issues arising, it is always beneficial to talk it out with your superiors and colleagues. Remember to remind yourself that everyone is unique and blessed with different opinions and thoughts. Embrace these differences. You should refrain yourself from being the target of rumours and gossips that may be caused by colleagues who may have it in for you and your relationship with your superior, client and other colleagues.

 **Relationships**

Unmarried couples should consider tying the knot in 2019, as fortune will favour Goat individuals and they will be blessed with a happy and prosperous marriage. Even without the help of Peach Blossom Luck star this year, single Goats are able to meet their potential partner. Thus, pay closer attention to the sign around you. Do not be afraid of going on potential dates with Mr. or Mrs. Right. Stay true to yourself and learn to love yourself first before learning to love someone else.

 **Health**

2019 is the year to focus more on your health and well-being. It is the year when you should eat accordingly and appropriately. Avoid heaty food, particularly fried food. Besides, it would be wiser to go for a lighter diet of food with less oil and more vegetables. Although there seems to be susceptibility to injuries and illnesses this year, they will not be anything major. Just remember to take time to take care of yourself.

 **Monthly Luck**

農曆正月 (February 4th - March 5th) 丙寅

Going by the rules, can never do you wrong. If you watch what you say and think of the potential consequences before you act or speak, you will be able to prevent any legal matters and unnecessary rumours and gossips from cropping up. Furthermore, you will experience some good times this month. So buy some wine and invite some friends over for a barbecue.

農曆二月 (March 6th - April 4th) 丁卯

This is the month when every Goat individual will gain benefit or two. Goats who are students, they will be eager to learn new things and will see a better potential to absorb information. Moreover, as for the others, they will have no trouble in executing plans, thus building up their savings and income for this month.

農曆三月 (April 5th - May 5th) 戊辰

A month of mix fortune is in store for you. There will be some bumps on the road, which will see a mixture of both good and bad days for you. That said, there is no reason to be overly alarmed. Prepare yourself well to face any potential situation and you will find ease in a well-stocked boat. Embrace the good times and enjoy the sun that shines through the stormy skies. This will be a well balance month for Goat individuals, so even when you are faced with a bad day, you will see the rainbow after a storm and the pot of gold with it.

農曆四月 (May 6th - June 5th) 己巳

Almost similar to previous months, this month would see average movement in terms of fortune for Goats. Likewise, white collar workers and students see some form of benefit from fortune. There is a big potential that white collar workers will face little to no difficulties at work thanks to their own perseverance while the latter will be able to gain more knowledge in school or college thus reaping better academic rewards.

農曆五月 (June 6th - July 6th) 庚午

An auspicious turn of fortune is in store for you. Goat individuals at work particularly, will find their business plans and outcomes work in their favour with lesser obstacles in their path. This would be a good month for mergers and building business corporations as these endeavours will bear amazing outcomes.

農曆六月 (July 7th - August 7th) 辛未

This month will see you practice your patience and attention to details. Though this month is littered with possible hurdles, being sprightly Goat individuals, you will still be able to use your little legs to jump over fences and trot over issues with great delicateness. That said, some word of advice would be to watch before you leap and measure every step with careful appraisal, to avoid any regrets this month.

農曆七月 (August 8th - September 7th) 壬申

Time spent with loved ones would be greatly restricted this month, thus be grateful for any time you get to have with them. Communicate well to gain their understanding as well as to know their feelings on any given situation. Communication is key in fostering any form relationship. Besides your lack of time spent with family and friends this month, you will also see an increase in workload. However, that is the essence of life and it is essential to treat any form of stress that arise from this increase in work as a lesson filed for life.

農曆八月 (September 8th - October 7th) 癸酉

Though faced with issues and stumbling blocks this month, Goat individuals are blessed with having protection from unlikely sources that will aid them when the need arises. When the going gets tough – do not panic as good tidings will arrive as soon as these stumbling blocks are cleared. Be patient and prepare yourself well for everything that is coming.

羊 The Goat in 2019

農曆九月 (October 8th - November 7th) 甲戌

Being attentive and vigilant are key practices for this month! You will experience some obstacles in things that you intend doing but they will not give you any major problem and these will be overcome. Having said that, this is definitely not the month to plan for that bungee jumping expedition you have wanted to try or booking yourself in for that sky diving adventure.

農曆十月 (November 8th - December 6th) 乙亥

All is well for you this month, as you will find yourself executing plans with ease and bravado. Unmarried Goats should pay attention to what (or who!) is around you this month, as your Mr. or Mrs. Right might be just around the corner from where you are. As a precaution, Goat individuals should avoid going out at night and to be wary when venturing out this month as the likelihood of something untoward occurring is high.

農曆十一月 (December 7th 2019 - January 5th 2020) 丙子

Some small aspects of monetary loss is unavoidable this month but fret not, there will be no major drop in your bank balance. This is another month to perhaps cash that negative down flow into some form of symbolic purchase for yourself. In this regard, the alignments suggest that any monetary loss you might experience, takes effect to block other potential negative elements that may be lurking around the corner.

農曆十二月 (January 6th - February 3rd 2020) 丁丑

More attention and focus should be placed on your health and wealth this month. As the saying goes, "Nothing looks as good as healthy feels", thus Goat individuals should watch what they eat, avoid excessive intake of unhealthy food and exercise regularly. Watch your savings this month and refrain from signing up and partaking in any form of investments, as the outcome of this may not work entirely in your favour.

Monkey 申

Year of the Monkey							
1920	1932	1944	1956	1968	1980	1992	2004

A person's Chinese age is obtained by adding one year to their Western birthday. For example, if you were born in 1976, your Western age in 2019 is 43, but your Chinese age would be 44.

Overall Forecast For The Year

申 2019 promises to be a fruitful year blessed with joyful occasions and good tidings. You have four auspicious Stars sending you boundless positive energy which you can use to your advantage. Although you will also have to contend with minor trials and tribulations this year, rest assured that you can overcome them all and sail through the year using the winds of good fortune blowing in your direction. Noble People will give you a little helpful nudge along the way.

You have a bright financial outlook in this Year of the Pig with the combined effects of the Jade Hall Star (玉堂) and Prosperity Star (福星). The Jade Hall Star indicates that this is an excellent time to grow your wealth. Your strengthening wealth luck is encouraging for asset acquisition; you may want to research or ask your friends for inside tips to invest in stocks or valuable properties. Your career is looking up this year with a possible promotion up the corporate ladder or a salary raise. If you are a business owner, you will get opportunities to expand your business and shore up your finances with the positive influence of this Star.

Further enhancing your good fortune this year is the Prosperity Star. This year, you will likely be presented with many opportunities to showcase your talents and impress your bosses. It's time to step up to the plate and take ownership for your work if you want to make significant progress in your career. Everything you wish for is within your reach – be it a big bonus or a promotion – but only if you put forth the effort and believe in yourself. Keep upgrading your skills and make the most of any chances you get to prove your worth at work, and you will be richly rewarded.

While you are enjoying your career high and achievements, there will be some negative consequences in the form of disputes and slander, or problematic interpersonal relationships. This is due to the presence of both the Curled Tongue (卷舌) and Crossing Sha (絞煞) Stars. You may find malicious gossip and lies about you flying around in your workplace or people envious about your success trying to entrap you in petty disputes to distract and undermine you. If you are not careful, some of these disputes could result in legal troubles. As much as possible, try to avoid these problematic people and do not engage with them. Keep to your inner circle of trusted friends and ignore what others say.

There is a price to pay for success; sometimes it can get quite lonely at the top. While you are flying high in your career, you may feel rather lonely and isolated due to the influence of the Six Harms Star (六害). The name of this Star suggests something quite threatening, but's not as bad as it sounds. You may feel a heightened sense of anxiety or worry about the worst case scenario in every situation, causing yourself much unnecessary stress and mental anguish. The more you worry, the more distorted your perception of reality will be.

Fortunately, you have the Heavenly Virtue Star (天德) on your side. Its positive energy gives you the ability to remove obstacles in your way and the commitment to do so. Whenever you are stuck in a difficult situation or feeling down, reach out to your friends, colleagues and family for support. You will find that many people are willing to come to your aid. They will also give you a reality check and help boost your spirits.

The Drapes Star (披麻) suggests that you might see some delays or setbacks in your plans this year. When things do not go according to plan, you might feel emotional turmoil or a sense of hopelessness. You will also be exposed to new influences this year. Be wary that some of these influences are negative and could lead you astray. The Robbery Sha Star (劫煞) indicates that your reputation will be at risk if you open yourself up to bad influences. Remember that not everybody has your best interests at heart. You will need to be more discerning to be able to tell your real friends apart from people who may have ulterior motives in getting close to you.

As the saying goes, there is a silver lining to every cloud. To mitigate the negative effects of the abovementioned Stars, you can draw upon the Nobleman Star (貴人) in your corner. This Star attracts mentors and Noble People into your life in times of need. When you have generous and kind people coming to your assistance or sharing their insights with you, you will find that your troubles are not so insurmountable after all. Having people to give you moral support as you tackle your life's challenges will lower your stress levels and make your victories taste even sweeter.

The Forecast for Individual Aspects of the Year

 **Wealth**

You have wealth luck this year, and it depends a lot on your resourcefulness and quick-wittedness in being able to make it work. Find ways to capitalise on your knowledge and learning to make your financial success grow. Remember, don't just think for the short-term, but consider your long-term goals for the years to come as well.

 **Career**

With help from noble people, you stand a good chance of getting promoted. But quick-tongued Monkeys must remember to always be gracious and humble, otherwise the people who are left behind in the rat race may be compelled to talk about you behind your back. They may resort to petty gossip and make their trivial resentments known, so the Monkey should strive to be accommodating and friendly or else this could cause some amount of stress for you. As the saying goes, "Life is a continuous learning process," and therefore you are advised to learn new things day by day and equip yourself with the necessary abilities for future career development. Do not be afraid to ask around should you need any help too.

The Monkey in 2019

 **Relationships**

Male Monkeys will see the greatest benefit of this year, while female individuals see average success in relationships. Hence, single male Monkeys need to be observant and start mingling around your social circle, as there is good chance of meeting that one person who is meant for you, so start asking people out for coffee! Couples that are already in love, wedding bells are on the horizon, so perhaps it's time to gear up to pop that once-in-a-lifetime question. Married female individuals will have average but stable marriage lives with their husbands in 2019.

 **Health**

A reasonable year for health, though Monkeys need to be wary about potential issues with their stomach. You must treat this as a gentle reminder to be extra cautious about what you eat and drink. Make that doctors appointment for your annual checkup and take extra care of your well-being to prevent unnecessary injuries. Aim for a healthier body by exercising regularly and eating properly in order to confront subtle health issues that might be in store for you.

 **Monthly Luck**

農曆正月 (February 4th - March 5th) 丙寅

This month will see you skating on thin ice. You will be bogged down by stressful work constraints that you might need to take special heed to. You will be faced with a higher workload this month, so take this as an opportunity to learn. Prepare yourself with various capabilities but be cautious of every move you make. Besides, always think before you act to avoid any costly decision.

農曆二月 (March 6th - April 4th) 丁卯

Though you will still be encountering some setbacks this month, your fortune will take a better auspicious turn from the previous month. So relax a little and enjoy the finer developments that your career and wealth plans will provide. Also, you will be blessed with more time spent with your family members, thus do go ahead to plan for more family outings in this month.

農曆三月 (April 5th - May 5th) 戊辰

All is well for you this month, and henceforth you will find yourself executing plans with great ease and dexterity. As a reward for all your endeavours, your fortune in career, wealth and relationship will see positive outcomes this month. This change of tidings will fruit positive effects into your life, so be ready to embrace them and bask in the fruits of your labour! As the saying goes, "You cannot do a good job, if your job is all you do." Therefore aim for a good work-life balance so as to not burn yourself out too fast.

農曆四月 (May 6th - June 5th) 己巳

Carrying over the good fortune from the previous month, most of your tasks will have great progress and you will see benefit in return. Monkeys are known to be highly intelligent and adaptable animals, thus with some help from the people around, Monkeys will be able to further develop their careers this month, gradually receiving more opportunities.

農曆五月 (June 6th - July 6th) 庚午

This month will see average movement in most areas of your life. White collar Monkeys will enjoy a rather smooth sailing month where you will see your superior and colleagues agree with your innovative. Furthermore, those that are in school will see more dedication and responsibility flowing within them.

農曆六月 (July 7th - August 7th) 辛未

Single Monkeys are advised to use this month to scout for potential love mates. He or she could be right around the block or possibly even under your very nose. Sign up for a singles event, or a meet up session in your local area that will expand your social circle and put you on the right path to meeting the one! Monkey individuals should also look after their health a little more, as they are susceptible to some minor illnesses. Pay attention to your well-being as this will propel you better in other areas as well.

農曆七月 (August 8th - September 7th) 壬申

In contrast to previous months, you will find yourself more fatigued than usual. But, as the saying goes, "Nothing worth having, comes easy", in order to reach your goals and achieve greater things, you will have to place more effort and time into your endeavours. In addition, Career driven Monkeys will be going through a month of average during this period of time.

農曆八月 (September 8th - October 7th) 癸酉

This month will take you on a fortune rollercoaster, and like a rollercoaster you will experience some ups and downs. Also, like being on a rollercoaster, this might cause you to feel a little out of control. To aid this period - be more detailed and attentive when dealing with your plans and day to day tasks. Stay grateful for everything you do, execute your plans with confidence, and the rest will take care of itself.

農曆九月 **(October 8th - November 7th)** 甲戌

You will see this month progressing a lot slower than the previous months. And sometimes slow is good as all good things take time to manifest. As the saying goes 'The longer the wait, the better the results'. Take your time in devising a good plan of outcome and be persistent in the changes you want to see in the relevant areas of your life.

農曆十月 **(November 8th - December 6th)** 乙亥

This month might need you to be a little more cautious in terms of health. Take extra care of your well-being to prevent unnecessary injuries. This year is also perhaps not the month to sign up for that parasailing adventure or scuba diving course, as there will be the likelihood of unavoidable mishaps. Your workload will see a little increase. You might find that your contributions might go unnoticed this month. Do not let this get to you, but rather work hard for your personal better development.

農曆十一月 **(December 7th 2019 - January 5th 2020)** 丙子

As a reward for all your endeavours, your fortune in career, wealth and relationship will see positive outcomes this month. The roller-coaster ride has reached its station and you can finally let that sigh of relief go, as things will move closer to your favour. So, get back on your path and run along to the finish line.

農曆十二月 **(January 6th - February 3rd 2020)** 丁丑

Your fortune takes another big step towards the auspicious end. Thus, be bold enough to nurture your career and make those financial plans a reality. They are likely to produce formidable outcomes. Allow yourself to a have a better-relaxed mind and body to embrace all the excitement that is coming your way this month.

Rooster 酉

Year of the Rooster							
1933	1945	1957	1969	1981	1993	2005	2017

A person's Chinese age is obtained by adding one year to their Western birthday. For example, if you were born in 1976, your Western age in 2019 is 43, but your Chinese age would be 44.

Overall Forecast For The Year

2019 is going to be an eventful year for you, as you will be experiencing some highs and lows in both your personal and professional life. Perseverance and persistence is all you need to deal with these challenges. Taken with an optimistic attitude, problems and challenges are tests of your mental fortitude and character. While being tested, you will learn what your strengths and weaknesses are. This year is especially good for personal development and academia.

Aligning with this is the Intelligence Star (文昌), which brings positive vibes for scholastic pursuits and exams. This is pertinent to those in the business of learning, research and academia. It also bodes well for people in the creative and administrative fields - whether you are a lecturer, college student, writer, musician, designer or researcher - to yield results and achieve excellence this year. You must not give up when faced with obstacles; even if you can't see the light at the end of the tunnel, keep moving forward and you will find the breakthrough that you have long been searching for. Focus on your goals and do not waver; success will arrive sooner than you think.

While you are exploring new paths and expanding your knowledge, take care of your personal belongings, especially when you travel. You may be susceptible to losing personal items and important documents due to the influence of the Solid Killing Star (的煞). Always make sure that your passport and valuables are with you when you get off a taxi or leave a restaurant. Try not to wear expensive jewelry while travelling to avoid theft. Likewise, do not leave too many valuables in your house, in case of a potential burglary when you're away. Store your important personal items and jewelry in a rented fix deposit box of a nearby bank instead.

Areas of communication may not go so smoothly for you this year, as suggested by the Broken Star (破碎). When there is a communication breakdown, false rumours about you could be spread by others, resulting in your diminished public image and reputation in your social circles. Be conscientious to notify your superiors at work about your plans and always keep an open line of communication with them. You can also adopt a more positive approach by listening better to what people say about you – both good and bad – and be humble to apologize if you are at fault and change your ways.

Other than that, you should be more vigilant about your personal safety when you are travelling, due to the influence of the Calamity Sha Star (災煞). This negative Star brings about an increased risk of injuries or accidents while travelling or on the move. Although you cannot completely avoid travel altogether, nor should you be overly paranoid about accidents occurring, you can always take sensible safety precautions such as not driving in bad weather and making sure that your car gets serviced regularly. Instead of taking short-cuts on a side road filled with potholes, take the highway instead. Never drive over the speed limit in a rush to get to your destination. You can avoid most accidents by eliminating unnecessary risks.

Additionally, you might want refrain from attending any funerals this year. This is because the combined presence of the Sky Dog Star and Funeral Guest Stars strongly indicates that if you were to attend such grim events this year, the negative energies present in these situations will have a negative impact on your own well-being. So, if you can opt out of attending a funeral, it would be wise to do so.

Overall, the Year of the Pig will be mainly be about learning and preparation for you. Use it wisely, and you can look forward to better things to come in the following year. Embrace changes and keep striving towards your goal even if you don't see immediate progress. Most of all, you should stay optimistic, so that you can find opportunities when faced with challenges. Remember that a pessimist sees the difficulty in every opportunity, while an optimist sees the opportunity in every difficulty. The difficulties that do not break you will only make you stronger.

The Forecast for Individual Aspects of the Year

Wealth

2019 will be a rather rocky year in terms of wealth. Therefore, it will be wise to keep your finances in check and curtail overspending. Despite the possible hit to your financials, there is no real reason to be overly concerned. Perhaps as a form of symbolic financial loss, place your money on some assets or perhaps purchase something you may have had your eye on. Exercise some patience for a short while as there will be periods of time when you will be able to carry through some financial plans that will allow some recovery from the earlier financial loss.

Career

This year will see you frazzled by stressful work expectations that you might take special heed to. You might see rising tensions with your superiors and it will be best to keep calm and level headed in any possible confrontation. Do not be disheartened by all these since stumbling blocks are built for you to leap to greater heights in life. Enhanced relationships with colleagues will allow them to start paying you more attention, which will subsequently give them the chance to appreciate the efforts that you pitch in as a team.

 **Relationships**

The year ahead does not bode well for the possibility of strong love developments for singleton Roosters looking for love. That said, there will be a few months where opportunities will favour you and where you may gather the courage to perhaps approach that person you have had your eye on. If you are not one to make the first move, perhaps, dropping some hints to show your keenness is a good start. For now it is better to be patient and go on dates when you feel that it is right. For those already in a relationship, this is the year to solidify and further the commitment.

 **Health**

To preserve your health and wellness this year, it would be best to avoid extreme and dangerous activities such as hiking or scuba diving. This year is also perhaps not the year to make that trek up Mt.Everest for that bucket list wish. Instead, opt for light exercises such as dancing, jogging and yoga. This will build your stamina and help get you to where you should be in terms of your general health. In the home, Rooster individuals are advised to position your furniture strategically so as to not cause any inconvenience to manoeuvring around the house.

 **Monthly Luck**

農曆正月 (February 4th - March 5th) 丙寅

Conditions will not run as smoothly as you may like it to, but this should not stop you from pouring in your efforts and giving everything you do a one hundred per cent. Roosters are known for their meticulous attention to details, and this can work in your favour to counter the current inauspicious direction and edge closer to the better end of things. You must be prudent at all times. Trust that every obstacle that you are currently experiencing now will peter out eventually.

農曆二月 (March 6th - April 4th) 丁卯

Roosters will see a heavier workload in various matters this month. You will need to keep an extra tight focus on projects delegated to you. It is also best to accept things as they are and work on issues on hand at hand step by step. If you need to make crucial decisions, perhaps seeking some assistance from the others may hold you to better favour.

農曆三月 (April 5th - May 5th) 戊辰

Months of hard-work will have trained you well and allowed you to become a better person this month. Therefore, let yourself relax a little and enjoy the fruits of your labour as an auspicious turn of fortune is in store for you! Furthermore, use this month to delve into things that you had put aside as you might see the good tidings of month ease you to findings solutions to problems that may have evaded you prior. Smile from time to time and enjoy life's brightest moment.

農曆四月 (May 6th - June 5th) 己巳

The saying, "Lesser the expectations, lesser the disappointment and more the surprise" is best to describe the mix of fortune that is coming your way this particular month. It is always best keep your expectations low to help ease the stresses from dealing with too many things. Though you might not be able to find as many solutions to problems, the help you receive will minimise your losses and guide you throughout this month.

農曆五月 (June 6th - July 6th) 庚午

In contrast to the previous month, your fortune will see a better turn this month. You will see a better chance at having a romantic relationship. Single Roosters should be more attentive to their surroundings as their soul mate might just be around the corner. It is always wise to be yourself when meeting new people and stay modest. These are the best ways to give a neutral first impression that will work in your favour. Nevertheless, married couples should work to foster closer bond with your spouse. This may help prevent any possible intrusion by an ill-intentioned third party.

農曆六月 (July 7th - August 7th) 辛未

Time spent with family is time well spent! A busy schedule is not an excuse not to spare some time for your family. When work is not all consuming, allow yourself to de-stress a little and spend that quality time with family. Go to a park or play sports together and foster better communication with each other. Likewise, stay alert while at work as you are a little more vulnerable to mistakes than the norm this month.

農曆七月 (August 8th - September 7th) 壬申

Paying attention to details is the key this month. Watch what you say and keep away from partaking in any unnecessary gossip. Be wary of potential legal issues that may crop up this month. Refrain from being the guarantor to anyone and be wary of signing any legally binding documents and agreements to avoid any negligent slipups that could possibly bring upon legal issues.

農曆八月 (September 8th - October 7th) 癸酉

When you are graced with modest opportunities to showcase your talent, getting ahead of yourself is the last thing you want this month. Instead, treat these opportunities as tests and a form of self-reflection to your true abilities. Keep your head grounded and focus on making the best of what has been dished to you.

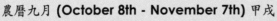

農曆九月 (October 8th - November 7th) 甲戌

Stumbling blocks in life are meant to be stepping stones for you to be a better person today than yesterday. Therefore, do not allow issues at hand to disturb you but instead channel them for better character building. This is also a good time to foster your relationship with the others. Try to pay more attention while communicating with people around you thus creating a better liveable environment.

農曆十月 (November 8th - December 6th) 乙亥

You will still come across certain setbacks this month, but you will also see a slight improvement from last month's rollercoaster. As Rooster individuals are blessed with intelligence and earnestness, with prolonged effort, these qualities will propel them to leap over hurdles and embrace the retribution of their hard work. This month, also prevent yourself getting into petty disputes. This is time to be generous!

農曆十一月 (December 7th 2019 - January 5th 2020) 丙子

As a reward for all your endeavours, your fortune in career, wealth and relationship will see positive outcomes this month. In order to have a healthy body to savour the sweetness your achievements and victory, allocate more focus towards your well-being. Adopt an exercise regime and diet plan that fits to your schedule and adhere strictly to it. A prepared mind and a healthy body will allow you to brace yourself for upcoming challenges.

農曆十二月 (January 6th - February 3rd 2020) 丁丑

Your focus on health matters must remain your steadfast priority this month. With your continuous effort to boost your well-being you will see better outcomes in terms of finances this month, thanks to that additional boost of energy. Nonetheless, in order to gain even better triumph, do not get ahead of yourself, rather, accumulate this success to further fuel your motivation to strive better in the future.

Dog 戌

Year of the Dog							
1934	1946	1958	1970	1982	1994	2006	2018

A person's Chinese age is obtained by adding one year to their Western birthday. For example, if you were born in 1976, your Western age in 2019 is 43, but your Chinese age would be 44.

Overall Forecast For The Year

戌 You can look forward to much growth and personal development in 2019. It is high time to slow down and take better care of your health if you've been taking it for granted. Keep a calm mind and don't react to provocations so that you won't be dragged into heated arguments with people around you. The good news is that there will be cause for celebrations and goodwill flowing throughout the year, so allow yourself to bask in some happiness while spending time with your loved ones. This is the year for renewal and rejuvenation of your body, mind and spirit.

As the Sky Sha Star (天煞) indicates, there will be potential delays and setbacks to your plans in the Year of the Pig. It's best to brace yourself with contingency plans and be prepared to make some necessary diversions. Be flexible and resourceful, and don't fret the small stuff. Sometimes, disappointments can be a blessing in disguise. When one door closes, another one opens. When things are not going according to plan, you must learn to find alternative solutions and pivot in a new direction. By overcoming these setbacks, you will realise that you are far more capable than you think.

On top of that, you might get embroiled in numerous quarrels throughout the year due to the influence of the Year Sha Star (歲煞). Perhaps you will have to get through difficult people at work, or live with housemates who are inconsiderate and selfish. Try to avoid confrontations and petty arguments if you can, as they will drain your energy. However, there will be times when you'll have to stand up for yourself or someone you care about. If you feel a sense of injustice about a situation, be assertive and confident in holding your ground. By keeping your integrity, others will learn to respect you.

Making your year even more challenging is the Surpassing Path Star (陌越) which heightens your tendency to be anxious or agitated when faced with stressful situations. You may find yourself in constant mental and emotional turmoil if you allow your problems to eat you up. Learn to relax and take the broader view of things. Worrying all the time and fearing the worst will only result in a gloomy self-fulfilling prophecy. Over time, you will be emotionally worn out and unable to think clearly. Force yourself to shut down those negative thoughts that pop into your mind and think positive thoughts instead. Having an optimistic mindset will not only make you more resilient in solving problems, it will also be beneficial to your emotional well-being.

When your mind and emotions are not at peace, your physical health will also be affected as they are all inter-connected. Be kind to yourself and treat your body well because the combined effects of the Yellow Flag Star (黄幡) and Sickness Charm Star (病符) suggest that you might have some serious health ailments this year if you don't take some time-out to recharge your batteries. You cannot keep filling other people's cups if your own cup is empty. Allow yourself to indulge in some rest and relaxation by going to a spiritual retreat, vacation or even volunteering at your favourite charity. Practise a healthy lifestyle by sticking to a balanced diet and getting enough sleep. Additionally, you could take up meditation or do some exercise that helps you to release all those pent-up emotions.

Another Star that may affect your emotions is the Lonesome Star (寡宿) which amplifies feelings of loneliness for Dog individuals this year. You may feel that you're unwanted or all alone in facing your struggles or that you're always misunderstood by everyone. This could cause you to detach yourself from others, so as to prevent yourself from getting hurt or disappointed by them. Don't be a Lone Ranger, as you have people who are close to you who care. Spend more time with your friends and family, and reach out to people whom you trust to talk about your frustrations. They will help to dispel your negativity and cheer you up.

On that note, this is a good year for happy events like marriage or graduation ceremonies as denoted by the Sky Happiness Star (天喜). There will be much to celebrate. Perhaps someone in your family will get married and you can build goodwill by helping to organize the event, whilst taking the opportunity to bond with your loved ones. The Star also indicates it's time to shine for those of you in academia and the knowledge industry. Show your capabilities at work and you could gain that promotion you've been waiting for. Lastly, there's a possible new addition to the family for those who are married and for those who are single, you may meet your Mr. or Mrs Right this year. Put on your best smile and go out there and mingle; you can't meet your match by staying at home!

The Forecast for Individual Aspects of the Year

 **Wealth**

This year will see fair fortunes in terms of wealth which will allow you to perform certain investment moves that you have long been planning. With a good tactical approach to finances, financial details will take care of themselves and work in favour of you. You will benefit greatly from the income flow to your bank account. In addition, 2019 is not a year that is predicted to fall in favour with your debtors and therefore you should try and use this opportunity to approach your debtors with little fear and perhaps attempt to clear away your last remaining debts with them.

 **Career**

The Dog will find itself dissatisfied and bored at work this year, and this could prompt you to get into arguments and disagreements with your colleagues. It may be hard to be efficient or productive in this kind of environment, but this is not good for you to make a significant career change. Therefore, attempt to make the best of it as the tide will soon turn.

 **Relationships**

Dog individuals will receive a great boost to their romantic lives in 2019. As for couples that are already in love, wedding bells are on the horizon, so perhaps it's time to gear up to pop that once-in-a-lifetime question. On the other hand, single Dogs need to be observant and start mingling around your social circle, as there is a good chance of meeting that one person who will shake your core soon. Also, for those of you who already have their eyes out for that someone, it's time to ask them out for coffee!

 **Health**

You might be faced with several signs of danger and illnesses lurking around in 2019. Overall attention and focus should be on your health to ward off potential ailments, though there will be no serious or major ramifications to this. While Dogs are known to be quick-witted and cool-headed, individuals should endeavour to achieve a healthier body and a cheerful mind by exercising regularly and eating properly in order to confront subtle health issues that might be in store for you.

 **Monthly Luck**

農曆正月 (February 4th - March 5th) 丙寅

This will be a pleasant month for you. Do not allow yourself to be restricted and do not place restrictions on yourself. Enjoy the month and the blessings that come with it. Though there might be some bumps on the road, you will receive the help you require from those around you. As an added icing on the cake, your wealth will experience significant allowing for greater allowance on monetary plans.

農曆二月 (March 6th - April 4th) 丁卯

This month will take you on a short curved road. There will be periods of when you will feel like a spinning cloth in a washing cycle and other times you will feel like you somewhat have things tethered together. Be more detailed and attentive when dealing with your plans and day to day tasks. You will find the means to the end of things by the month's end.

農曆三月 (April 5th - May 5th) 戊辰

This would be a rocky month in terms of financial health. It will be wise to keep your finances in balance and perhaps curtail overspending. As a form of symbolic financial loss, draw your money towards purchases of assets or some desired necessity. As tidings for your well-being is ill placed this month, it would be best to avoid extreme and dangerous adventures such as hiking or scuba diving.

農曆四月 (May 6th - June 5th) 己巳

Peach Blossom Luck is in sight this month! Single Dogs are advised to use this month to keep an eye out for potential love mates. He or she could be right around the block or even under your very nose. Head on out for a singles event, or a meet and greet session in your local café that will expand your social circle and put you on the right path to meeting the one! However, a note of caution to both committed and married couples - cut down on one to one interactions with the opposite sex this month. This might safeguard your relationship from a third party interference.

農曆五月 (June 6th - July 6th) 庚午

You will have good reasons to be grateful this month as excellent luck is expected. This change of tidings will bring fruitful positive effects into your life, so be ready to embrace them and bask in the fruits of your labour! Work hard and put your best foot forward to gain the attention of your superiors. When recognition is given, you will probably find yourself at the receiving end of a salary increment.

農曆六月 (July 7th - August 7th) 辛未

You will be granted more time to spend with your friends this month. Do not refrain yourself from socialising too much. Part and parcel of having a good and balanced life is the added social life. Head out for good food or a decent buffet or spend your weekend with your peers. Allow yourself these little treats to de-stress and spend that quality time with your friends. After all they are second to family.

農曆七月 (August 8th - September 7th) 壬申

Anticipate a not-so-good month of luck. This might present itself in the form of workload which would cause you to be a little more tired than usual at work. To overcome this, allow yourself to rest more whenever there is time to do so. Head up to your preferred bookstore and pick up a book or sign up for a good gym. The flush of endorphins will allow you to feel better. On the bright side, your fortune in other areas of life, such as wealth, health and relationship will see better movement this month.

農曆八月 (September 8th - October 7th) 癸酉

It is time to put more attention on your hygiene this month. Yes it's time to pick that toothbrush. Wash your clothes regularly, shower frequently and tidy up your wardrobe as a clean and tidy appearance will give you a refreshing approach to various matters. Having said that, Dog individuals shall not be too adventurous when it comes to food intake this month. Cut down on that grease and seasoning for a little bit to prevent any illness setting you in its sight.

農曆九月 (October 8th - November 7th) 甲戌

This is another month to refrain from any extreme or dangerous activities such as skateboarding or white water rafting as Dog individuals are vulnerable to both minor and major injuries and illnesses this month. Adopt a different approach to finding things to do in your spare time. Perhaps, sign up for an interesting courses that will also help you in expanding your career, or head on down to that jazz bar with friends you have been meaning to go to. Variety is the spice of life. While your prospects in other areas are excellent, hurting and wounding yourself is definitely the last thing you want!

農曆十月 (November 8th - December 6th) 乙亥

Your wealth will see you go through a roller coaster ride this month. To deal with the ups and downs in your finances, stay cool headed and remain calm. Money comes and goes, but it is the lessons that we have gained that will aid us in not repeating the same moves or mistakes. Likewise, your career, will be greatly aided by the Noblemen, as they will guide you throughout this period and therefore you might see the ease of these issues being resolved quickly.

農曆十一月 (December 7th 2019 - January 5th 2020) 丙子

Designers in particular, will see ideas coming into their heads faster than they can even process them. This fast paced thinking will allow you to splash your creative juices over a wide range of innovative concepts. Furthermore, fortune also favours other individuals for a flourishing career development this month. Therefore, one should go ahead to execute their undertakings at work to the best of their ability. Last but not least, junior Dogs should see a more determined version of themselves in the school environment. Do your homework regularly and you will be blessed with notable improvement.

農曆十二月 (January 6th - February 3rd 2020) 丁丑

An inauspicious turn of fortune from the previous month. There will be certain issues that will deter you from reaching your intended goals, therefore work assignments will not be easily completed on time. To resolve these issues, perhaps adopting a different strategic approach might work to your benefit. Adopt better courage and a never-say-die attitude. If Dog individuals are persistent enough, setbacks will be cleared away faster than they can appear.

Personalised Forecast For 2019 Based on Day of Birth

(Assessment based on the 60 Jia Zi 甲子 Day Pillars)

甲子 Jia Zi Day

Overview

A sweet and smooth sailing year in terms of career are in store for you! Nevertheless, this is not a time when you should lower down your guards. Avoid being too relax and keep your hard work going. Also, use your leisure and spare time to enrol into certain programme or courses to stay afresh and motivated. These participation will sharpen your original skillsets and equip yourself with new capabilities. Furthermore, never involve yourself in reputation and fame pursuit this year.

 ## Wealth

This year, long-term investments are more favouring you compared to the short-term ones. Therefore, think long and hard about where you money goes to. Choose the firm options with excellent return namely property and higher education. Long term investments may require high patience and slower process, but it works multiple times better than investments with low and unstable returns.

 ## Relationships

Third party persons may intrude to your relationship due to jealousy. As such, practice your caution from time to time to avoid taking things for granted and underappreciate the effort of your partner. Stay attentive to every detail in relationship matters to avoid unnecessary issues. Besides, work on your communication skills and discuss issues with your partner in a calm mode to smoothen romance fortune.

 ## Health

Your eyes and heart are the health concerns that you should watch out of this year. Furthermore, you shall take this period of time to reschedule your exercise, diet and health habits. Set boundaries for healthier diets and coupled these routines with appropriate exercise habit that sustain your wellbeing throughout the year.

Career

Overall, your career are mostly favouring and auspicious this year. This can be seen in the form of plenty opportunities to enrich your professional capabilities. Nonetheless, never get ahead of yourself with your valuable traits. Stay modest and down to earth at all times.

農曆正月

(February 4th - March 5th) 丙寅
Despite the fact that good wealth fortune is in store for you this month, you shall control yourself from overspending, particularly those who are born in autumn season.

農曆二月

(March 6th - April 4th) 丁卯
As you reap as you sow, discipline and focus shall be dedicated to fruit rewards such as extra income.

農曆三月

(April 5th - May 5th) 戊辰
Overthinking and overanalysing are expected in you.

農曆四月

(May 6th - June 5th) 己巳
Fierce competition are heating up between you and your colleagues this month. Stay alert at all times as the others may make effort to steal your ideas away and make them theirs.

農曆五月

(June 6th - July 6th) 庚午
There are several career changes namely new superior in this month. Stay true to yourself and leave a good impression as this professional relationships helps develop your career growth.

農曆六月

(July 7th - August 7th) 辛未
One will come across cooperation and collaboration opportunities with others this month. Allocate more time on developing new ideas and discuss them with your co-workers.

農曆七月

(August 8th - September 7th) 壬申
Chances are you may encounter some accidents this month. Having said that, be extra cautious and careful whether you're driving on the road or walking down the street.

農曆八月

(September 8th - October 7th) 癸酉
You are apt to annoyance and hot temper this month. Now, don't be too harsh on yourself, calm down and think appropriately. You will be able to prevent heated conversations.

農曆九月

(October 8th - November 7th) 甲戌
Brace yourself for sudden changes, for both style and pace at work this month. You are expected to adapt quickly to whatever that your boss is throwing at you.

農曆十月

(November 8th - December 6th) 乙亥
Long term investments are not favouring you this month.

農曆十一月

(December 7th 2019 - January 5th 2020) 丙子
Pay attention while driving or walking on the street. Obey the traffic rules to prevent penalty.

農曆十二月

(January 6th - February 3rd 2020) 丁丑
Though your boss might not be able to deliver their promises, you shouldn't allow the dismays to become career distraction. Focus on you work, fortune will change for the better.

六十甲子

Forecast for 2019 based on Day of Birth

乙丑 Yi Chou Day

Overview

As you will be facing unforeseen challenges in the coming year, you have to remain steadfast and stand on your ground. When the time comes, you must be able to react without hesitation. Procrastinating should be avoided as well. When you're managing your schedule, try not to juggle too many things at the same time as it would cause you to lose focus, making it harder for you to achieve your goals.

 ## Wealth

Financial growth is in the bag only if you put effort into it. Whatever opportunities that comes your way, it might be wasted if you hesitate or let others take it. While you should put yourself first, it's not an excuse to mistreat others for your own success. Try to find the balance between looking out for yourself and at the same time having a healthy relationship with other people.

 ## Relationships

Family members will be particularly difficult to handle, especially your mother and a possible romantic interest. When trying to overcome these difficulties, practice caution and diplomacy. For men who are in relationships, chances are the relationship problems you will be facing stems from your girlfriend overtaking your status in terms of career and social network.

Health

Your physical health is looking good though you may suffer leg injuries this year. Additionally, your stomach and eyes may cause you problems as well. In order to prevent any issues related to your digestion, try adopting a healthier diet.

Career

The best way for you to flourish in your career this year would be your learning speed. Pick up a new skill or learn new knowledge that would be beneficial to your work. Work hard towards your goals at a steady pace in a process of continuous improvement.

農曆正月

(February 4th - March 5th) 丙寅
There's a possibility that you might get yourself tangled with the law this month, particularly if you drive often. On the road, be mindful of the rules and be on your best behaviour.

農曆二月

(March 6th - April 4th) 丁卯
In this month, you are required to put in the effort and time to earn your wealth. Any substantial financial gain won't come easy without the necessary work.

農曆三月

(April 5th - May 5th) 戊辰
If you try to make yourself recognised this month, chances are it won't be a fruitful endeavour. Seek to improve the quality of your work instead for a bigger pay-off later on.

農曆四月

(May 6th - June 5th) 己巳
Expect rivalry to thrive this month and play the game well in order to stay relevant.

農曆五月

(June 6th - July 6th) 庚午
Your superior might not give you the acknowledgement you want but take this experience as a lesson and see how you can come out of this as a better person.

農曆六月

(July 7th - August 7th) 辛未
There will be negative influences all around you this month that would drain your energy and take away your motivation. Unless you do your best to stay fresh and energetic, your work might be affected.

農曆七月

(August 8th - September 7th) 壬申
In this month, there's a big possibility for you to travel. At the same time, you may also be afflicted with food poisoning.

農曆八月

(September 8th - October 7th) 癸酉
Competition continues to grow at your workplace. Handle this wisely and be diplomatic with your colleagues.

農曆九月

(October 8th - November 7th) 甲戌
Practice the caution on your individual documents and property this month as there are risk lurking around them.

農曆十月

(November 8th - December 6th) 乙亥
If you were born in autumn, you can expect this month to be good as you may receive some form of career advancement.

農曆十一月

(December 7th 2019 - January 5th 2020) 丙子
Be mindful of the law in your endeavours. If you seek to take any shortcuts or cut corners, you will pay dearly for it if it breaks the rules.

農曆十二月

(January 6th - February 3rd 2020) 丁丑
This month, you might find yourself to be the target of baseless rumours. Do your best to avoid these petty people and instead focus on your goals.

丙寅 **Bing Yin Day**

Overview
An auspicious year awaits as you finally receive the recognition for all your efforts, resulting in more opportunities. Your performance at work would be satisfactory enough to earn you promotions or career advancements from your bosses. The future looks bright for you so continue putting in the hard work.

 ## Wealth
Financially speaking, your wealth is average. However, the respect and recognition at your workplace would open doors in the future. With the reputation you're building up where you are now, it's a basis for future endeavours that would bring about more wealth. Use it to your advantage by establishing networks with people who matter so you can benefit financially from this in the future.

 ## Relationships
For single women who's looking for love, you need to get yourself out there and actually look. Being passive is not a strategy to go for if you want results. For single men, romantic opportunities are out there, specifically in the first, second, eleventh and twelfth month. Don't be too dismissive of your choices and who knows, they might prove to be a match for you. Take the first step.

 ## Health
This year, be careful with your upper torso area as it's prone to injury. Seek immediate medical attention if there are negative signs in the area before it gets worse. You might find yourself susceptible to bone-related injuries as well so try to be more careful wherever applicable.

 ## Career
Career-wise, you're moving up the ladder this year; especially for those born in spring or winter. All the effort you have put in your work will finally be noticed so keep it up.

農曆正月

(February 4th - March 5th) 丙寅
This month, you'll find yourself with good financial luck. You might even be surprised with some financial reward that you didn't expect.

農曆二月

(March 6th - April 4th) 丁卯
The financial luck from the previous month continues. You may want to consider asking your superior for a pay raise.

農曆三月

(April 5th - May 5th) 戊辰
You're really on a roll with this good luck of yours as it spans into this month as well. Looks like you might get promoted or advance in your career.

農曆四月

(May 6th - June 5th) 己巳
Positive romance luck is in the air for the single ladies this month. If you're looking for love, take the initiative and make the first step to make it happen.

農曆五月

(June 6th - July 6th) 庚午
There may be problems at home as you find yourself dealing with a lot of disagreements. Practice patience and try to be understanding when you handle them.

農曆六月

(July 7th - August 7th) 辛未
At times, you will be tempted to impulsively spend beyond your budget. Try to curb this habit and be stricter when it comes to your wealth management.

農曆七月

(August 8th - September 7th) 壬申
If ever you feel like travelling, now's a good month. Consider going to places where you've always wanted to see with your own eyes.

農曆八月

(September 8th - October 7th) 癸酉
Your social life will experience a boom this month. Your network will grow larger and you will be swept up in parties and gatherings. However, you should refrain overindulging in alcohol.

農曆九月

(October 8th - November 7th) 甲戌
For those who were born in summer, they'll be plagued with stress this month. On the other hand, those born in spring will have their talents recognized and enjoy good fortune.

農曆十月

(November 8th - December 6th) 乙亥
This month unlocks your creative talents to its full potential, allowing you to breath in new life to old projects. Give a brand-new twist to an old concept.

農曆十一月

(December 7th 2019 - January 5th 2020) 丙子
There may be an increase in profit for you coming from good business prospects. Make your preparations now so that when the time comes, you will be ready for it.

農曆十二月

(January 6th - February 3rd 2020) 丁丑
As your financial luck is looking good this month, consider doing some investments.

丁卯 Ding Mao Day

Overview

By having recognition and gaining endorsement from your colleagues at work, you can expect your professional career to advance. In turn, your financial aspect would improve as well. To do so, don't be afraid to display your talents and capabilities to allow others to notice what you bring to the table. Have your eyes on the prize by following through your plan of action. If you keep this up, your efforts will eventually be rewarded.

 ## Wealth

You will find that money and reputation will come easy for you this year as you're more likely to be noticed than usual. As you appear more prominently on the radar, your network would increase and you will be in touch with more contacts; which would bring more financially-rewarding opportunities.

 ## Relationships

For those who are in a long-term relationship, it's high time to make it official and tie the knot. Single women who are still looking for Mr. Right have a good chance to become a Mrs. this year. But if you're already married, watch out for potential extramarital temptations.

 ## Health

Overall, your health will be good for this year. However, it's still important to take care of yourself in order to maintain this good health, especially if you're over sixty years old. This can be done with regular exercise, medical check-ups to monitor for any irregularities as some health issues pertaining your digestive system might appear.

 ## Career

Expect smooth sailing in your career with an abundance of stepping stones that would allow you to reach new heights. For this to be realized, it is up to you to be more proactive in grabbing the opportunities as you see them.

農曆正月

(February 4th - March 5th) 丙寅
Good wealth luck for this month overall. It would be wise to make the most of it by seeking out new opportunities and handle them in an efficient manner.

農曆二月

(March 6th - April 4th) 丁卯
In this month, you will find yourself in disagreements with people over financial issues. It's best to keep your head clear when you try to solve your predicament.

農曆三月

(April 5th - May 5th) 戊辰
It is important to organize the tasks you receive at work and differentiating them from your other professional obligations in order to minimize the risk of unnecessary misunderstanding.

農曆四月

(May 6th - June 5th) 己巳
This month, play it safe as you're more prone to get entangled with legal problems.

農曆五月

(June 6th - July 6th) 庚午
Put aside some of your spending and make sure you know exactly where your money is going, as there is a chance for a sudden financial loss to occur.

農曆六月

(July 7th - August 7th) 辛未
Your may find your relationship or marriage more rocky than usual due to money issues.

農曆七月

(August 8th - September 7th) 壬申
This is the month where you're likely to advance in your career. For single women, it's a great month as well because you are likely to find a great match around this time.

農曆八月

(September 8th - October 7th) 癸酉
If you find yourself on the road this month, avoid trouble. There's a chance for you to break the law and receive unnecessary penalty.

農曆九月

(October 8th - November 7th) 甲戌
Words have consequences and as such be mindful of what you speak. This is especially so for women.

農曆十月

(November 8th - December 6th) 乙亥
In this month, you seriously need to get some rest. Give yourself a break and take good care of yourself more.

農曆十一月

(December 7th 2019 - January 5th 2020) 丙子
This month, you will be inspired to create some great ideas which can be put to good use at work.

農曆十二月

(January 6th - February 3rd 2020) 丁丑
Pay attention to your health, particularly your stomach for this month.

戊辰 Wu Chen Day

Overview

In terms of wealth, a prosperous year awaits you. Focus on expanding your social network and learn how to make the best use of it to achieve your goals. In your endeavours, you might be hampered by false accusations and baseless rumours especially for those born in spring. Stay true to your goals and ignore these petty issues.

 ## Wealth

The opportunities that you find this year would originate from your social circles. By being more proactive in socialising, you may increase your professional standing. While you're looking to make a considerable amount of money, do practice caution when it comes to investments and go for more reliable avenues such as property.

 ## Relationships

For men, it will be an auspicious Peach Blossom Luck this year which may translate to marriage. Women on the other hand would not experience the same luck. If your love life is not as you hope it to be, there are other aspects of your life that you can work on to improve your overall happiness.

 ## Health

Be careful with your heart and eyes for the next two years. For this year, you may be afflicted by fever frequently so do take care of yourself to make sure your health is uncompromised. You might also find yourself easily tired this year.

 ## Career

Travelling for work-related reasons would help you in your career advancement. An example would be taking on outstation assignments. You might be feeling that you are being taken advantage of by your superior and burdened by work. But, these frustrations are merely temporary as the rewards that you would eventually gain are long-lasting.

農曆正月

(February 4th - March 5th) 丙寅
You can expect some good news this month especially for those born during autumn or winter. There's a possibility for you to gain some wealth too.

農曆二月

(March 6th - April 4th) 丁卯
In this month, travelling would be beneficial to your wealth so get yourself out there. You can also take this opportunity to relax from the work-related stress.

農曆三月

(April 5th - May 5th) 戊辰
In this month, there's a chance to find a new job. Before deciding anything, think your options through carefully as this change would affect your life adversely.

農曆四月

(May 6th - June 5th) 己巳
Extra focus and effort is needed this month when it comes to work. Practice discipline especially if you were born during winter.

農曆五月

(June 6th - July 6th) 庚午
This month you would not be in short of inspiration. The catch is you need to organise these new ideas well in order to fully utilise them.

農曆六月

(July 7th - August 7th) 辛未
You might find yourself being envious of others but that's just how things are. Be more appreciative of what you have instead.

農曆七月

(August 8th - September 7th) 壬申
Be mindful of your diet this year or you might run into some health problems such as stomach flu or food poisoning.

農曆八月

(September 8th - October 7th) 癸酉
You might be affected by heart-related troubles this month and this is particularly true if you are older. Make the necessary preparations and make sure you try to minimise this trouble.

農曆九月

(October 8th - November 7th) 甲戌
For those who own a business or supervising anyone, there may be problems concerning your staff that needs your attention. This includes household staff.

農曆十月

(November 8th - December 6th) 乙亥
You might be quite careless with the words you use this month. Keep that in mind and your head cool to avoid making any cutting remarks that would cause offence.

農曆十一月

(December 7th 2019 - January 5th 2020) 丙子
It will be beneficial for you to travel southwards this month. You also shouldn't be working alone for your wealth can be greatly improved through collaborations.

農曆十二月

(January 6th - February 3rd 2020) 丁丑
Take the time to spend with your family as much as possible because they may have felt neglected.

己巳 Ji Si Day

Overview

Overall, this year would be good for you particularly regarding your wealth luck. Rather than working for yourself or owning a business, you'll have better luck being employed instead. It would be favourable for you to try out something new or adopt a new hobby. Diversifying your talent now would be beneficial for you in the long run.

 ## Wealth

For your hard work, there's a possibility that it will be rewarded though an increment of salary. This increase however is subtle where it steadily rises with every thoughtful step you take. You may not see it immediately as it doesn't come in one lump sum, but it would be noticeable in the bigger picture. Additionally, risky investments ought to be avoided.

 ## Relationships

When it comes to relationships, men in particular would have to deal with meddling from their mothers this year. Between her and your partner, you should serve as the middle ground to minimize the friction. As for those who have been in relationships for a while, it's a good time this year to finally tie the knot.

 ## Health

This year you can expect to have good health in general. Having said that, it's something that ought to be maintained by living healthily. There's a chance that you might be afflicted by minor issues related to your digestive system and your stomach if you don't watch your diet.

 ## Career

A lot of growth can be expected of your career this year. Your hard work is finally bearing fruits. It would also be beneficial for you to pick up new skills or do whatever it takes to contribute towards boosting your professional reputation.

農曆正月

(February 4th - March 5th) 丙寅
Do not be afraid to stand your ground and speak up for what is right and what you want. You certainly deserve some recognition and reward, especially in your career.

農曆二月

(March 6th - April 4th) 丁卯
There might be risks of complication for pregnant women this month so they ought to take good care of their physical wellbeing.

農曆三月

(April 5th - May 5th) 戊辰
Procrastination should be avoided. Remain steadfast in your productivity and make sure all tasks are completed on time. Make a schedule and stick to it.

農曆四月

(May 6th - June 5th) 己巳
People might try to pull you into their petty conflict this month but don't let what they say get to you. If you participate in their drama, you might end up as a part of someone else's gossip and cause you unnecessary trouble.

農曆五月

(June 6th - July 6th) 庚午
This month, support and help would come easy from the opposite sex for you. Receive their help with gratitude and humility. Try not to be surprise when they offer you their help.

農曆六月

(July 7th - August 7th) 辛未
You might be having some health problems this month stemming from your stomach. Mood swings would follow soon after so try to mitigate the whole problem by being careful with what you eat.

農曆七月

(August 8th - September 7th) 壬申
It will be quite a troubling month for you. You should be aware that making the right choice is not something that is easily discernible. Look at the overall picture and think carefully before making any decision.

農曆八月

(September 8th - October 7th) 癸酉
This month, don't let impulse dictate your choices and decision. Your pride might demand irrational things from you but try to put it aside and see things as they truly are.

農曆九月

(October 8th - November 7th) 甲戌
Your burdens can be lessened this month through collaborating with others this month. Your work would then flow smoothly and your financial problems eased.

農曆十月

(November 8th - December 6th) 乙亥
For those in business or entrepreneurs, you might want to consider overseas to find new opportunities as they would bring great results this month.

農曆十一月
(December 7th 2019 - January 5th 2020) 丙子
Social obligations might shackle you this month. With it, you might be tempted to go overboard with alcohol and food so try to practice some restrain.

農曆十二月

(January 6th - February 3rd 2020) 丁丑
If you're a single woman looking for love, this month brings better luck in finding your ideal partner. Be more assertive and make the first move.

庚午 Geng Wu Day

Overview

This year, you will be met with many pleasant surprises. When it comes to career opportunities, it will come from your social and professional networks. These opportunities would have been out of reach if not through your contacts. At the same time, you might find yourself exhausted from the social aspect this year. Remember that you don't have to participate in every single social activity out there. Every now and then, set sometime for yourself and relax.

 ## Wealth

Working solo might have the benefit of being independent, but your goals are easier to achieve with the help of others; especially if you were born in autumn or winter. Try not to dabble in investments as it might be unfavourable. If you still wish to do so, go for the ones with minimal risks with long term return.

 ## Relationships

It's a good year for those in relationships to strengthen the bond they have with each other. However, trivial disagreements might spiral out of control if neither side can put their ego aside. Practice open and honest communication and be patient with each other.

 ## Health

Pay attention to the amount of sugar you consume. In general, stomach-related issues can be expected. These problems can be avoided by taking preventive measures in adopting a healthier diet.

 ## Career

When looking for inspiration related to your work, consider traveling. The new experiences will expand your field of thought. There's a chance that you would change jobs as well. Before you decide on anything, make sure you see through all your possible options. Change might be uncomfortable but don't be afraid of it.

農曆正月

(February 4th - March 5th) 丙寅

If you were born in summer, you might find some trouble in getting recognition from your boss. Your boss might even display favour towards your colleagues over you.

農曆二月

(March 6th - April 4th) 丁卯

This month, an offer for you to change jobs might appear. New wealth opportunities await should you take up on this offer. At the same time, consider all your options thoroughly before making your decision.

農曆三月

(April 5th - May 5th) 戊辰

At work and at your home you will be met with turmoil. Despite of this, don't be disheartened and stay calm. Disagreements and arguments are unavoidable, but what you can do about it is not let it fester and worsen.

農曆四月

(May 6th - June 5th) 己巳

At work, you will receive additional stress this month. If you get the chance travel northwards for work, take it as it would be favourable for you.

農曆五月

(June 6th - July 6th) 庚午

There's a possibility that you will be given a new responsibility. This is something you should put your very best into as a successful completion will greatly progress your career.

農曆六月

(July 7th - August 7th) 辛未

Mind your temper this month as your emotions run wild. You might say or do something you will regret out of anger. While these emotional outbursts are temporary in nature, the damage they can inflict could be lasting.

農曆七月

(August 8th - September 7th) 壬申

In terms of wealth, you're getting better this month. To secure your current improved financial standing, maintain good discipline in your finances.

農曆八月

(September 8th - October 7th) 癸酉

Other people might give you their opinion and criticism, and you should cast aside your ego to give them your consideration. The ideas that they offer might be beneficial for you, particularly in terms of your finances.

農曆九月

(October 8th - November 7th) 甲戌

Stress at work is to be expected. Every now and then, make sure you give yourself some time off to reinvigorate your spirit.

農曆十月

(November 8th - December 6th) 乙亥

There's a chance this month for your stomach to cause you problems, especially if you're travelling north. Watch what you eat and practice good hygiene.

農曆十一月

(December 7th 2019 - January 5th 2020) 丙子

In regards to your relationship issues, those close to you might chime in to offer you advice. It would be up to you to discern which advice is applicable and which to take with a grain of salt.

農曆十二月

(January 6th - February 3rd 2020) 丁丑

The secret to a happy marriage would be trust and honesty. Those who are married should practice this when they disagree with one another. Have open communication between both parties to dispel any distrust that might harm the relationship.

辛未 **Xin Wei Day**

Overview

A wealthy year is in store for you as there will be plenty opportunities present. Your time to strive hard and explore for new openings is here since you will not be bothered by worrying business decisions. Your fortune is greatly auspicious as even spontaneous actions will fruit excellent results. Utilize this year to move forth and work for the great start in life.

 Wealth

Spring season babies will be blessed with capital gain this year. Stay prepared and attentive to incoming openings to fully utilize your chances. Over-suspiciousness and hesitation will only disrupt your motivation, losing out significant openings as a result.

 Relationships

For male individuals that are in long-term relationships, you might want to consider about tying the knot this year. As for married men, prioritize your endeavours on your romance life over the other areas to further enrich the relationship between you and your spouse. Spend time and effort for your partner.

 Health

For those that were born in summer or autumn seasons, you will encounter declined health condition. Make wellbeing your primary concern and take care of yourself appropriately. Refrain from taking things for granted or even seek for momentary happiness.

 Career

Facilitated work growth due to your persistent effort and contribution can be seen in the form of promotion or increment. Also, your career reputation will be blossomed as a result.

農曆正月

(February 4th - March 5th) 丙寅
This is a month which favours teamwork building at your workplace. Talk your experience and feelings with your peers and you will find work more pleasant than it was.

農曆二月

(March 6th - April 4th) 丁卯
It is auspicious for you to take on new roles and tasks in your career this month. For those who are particularly born in the spring, things will work even smoother in your way.

農曆三月

(April 5th - May 5th) 戊辰
Excellent wealth fortune are in store for those who were born in the spring or winter. On the other hand, the others will feel vice versa.

農曆四月

(May 6th - June 5th) 己巳
Facilitated work growth can be seen in the form of increment or promotion. However, one shall first prove oneself on whether one deserve such opening by being a persistent and hard worker.

農曆五月

(June 6th - July 6th) 庚午
Career changes in the form of new superiors are in sight for you! They will perform various new plans and arrangements which will do nothing but good to the company.

農曆六月

(July 7th - August 7th) 辛未
Those born in the summer or autumn seasons will particularly feel the tension at workplace. Communicate properly to avoid any disputes and arguments.

農曆七月

(August 8th - September 7th) 壬申
Hot temper may cause you to raise arguments this month. Thread and act carefully while liaising with the others to avoid any disputes.

農曆八月

(September 8th - October 7th) 癸酉
You're bearing heavier responsibilities on your shoulders. Take a step back and verify where your obligation really lies on. Only then you may design solution to tackle these issues.

農曆九月

(October 8th - November 7th) 甲戌
Do not be unconcerned over matters this month. If you are not careful enough, chances are you will waste more valuable time for unnecessary issues or mess.

農曆十月

(November 8th - December 6th) 乙亥
Never judge a book by its cover because all that you've seen might just be the tip of an iceberg. Some colleagues may camouflage themselves with kindness, so you should beware of their ulterior intentions.

農曆十一月

(December 7th 2019 - January 5th 2020) 丙子
Unavoidable financial loss is inevitable as you will be spending a big amount of money for the senior members of your family.

農曆十二月

(January 6th - February 3rd 2020) 丁丑
Your worries and uneasiness are due to feeling of being taken advantage by the others who are highly dependent on you. Be honest with how you feel and seek solution to solve the issues.

壬申 Ren Shen Day

Ren
申
Shen

Overview

A challenging year awaits you. Worry not as you would be able to see things through by having back up plans for worst case scenarios. Once this period of difficulty is through, you will come out of it as a better person and learn a thing or two. If you have any problems with your boss, this year it may get worse. Regardless of your current situation, try to be patient and stay put. Now is not the time for you to change jobs.

 ## Wealth

Your efforts should be in maintaining what you have through careful budgeting. It would not be good for you to be involved in risky or hasty investments as they would not bring you any benefit. Be smart with how you handle your finances.

 ## Relationships

For those who are married, they need to be strong for each other. Honour relationship by staying faithful to your partner. For those who are single, it's better to focus on other aspects of their life besides relationship as it is not the right time for romance.

 ## Health

What would afflict you this year is more emotional than physical, manifesting itself as stress. Otherwise, your health is alright. While you may be troubled by mental turmoil, go for relaxing physical activities to reduce the negative energy. It wouldn't hurt to go for regular medical check-ups as well.

 ## Career

At work, you may feel unappreciated and you're looking for recognition. This might lead you to consider a change of job but refrain from that decision. It's not a good time for you to do so yet, so focus on your current job for the moment and try to secure your current position first.

農曆正月

(February 4th - March 5th) 丙寅
As you feel that you are unappreciated by your superiors at work, you may run into some problems out of this.

農曆二月

(March 6th - April 4th) 丁卯
For those born during summer, misfortune would have a greater effect on them this month. Be more adaptive and perhaps things would improve for you.

農曆三月

(April 5th - May 5th) 戊辰
This month, you may be faced with problems in finding inspiration. Don't let the frustration get the better of you. Stay focused in your tasks and soldier on to ensure that your workload won't accumulate and become a bigger burden for you in the future.

農曆四月

(May 6th - June 5th) 己巳
Not much progress is expected of this month as stagnation continues. You will remain inactive. Take this opportunity to do some introspection and keep your options open on how to make your situation better.

農曆五月

(June 6th - July 6th) 庚午
It will be productive month for those working in artistic and creative industries. You will be able to work better and faster thanks to a boost in inspiration.

農曆六月

(July 7th - August 7th) 辛未
Consider giving yourself some time off this month. While you're at it, take good care of your health as you may injure your right leg.

農曆七月

(August 8th - September 7th) 壬申
This month, your wealth luck is looking to improve but don't let it get to your head as you may decide wrongly on certain things that would have you worse off.

農曆八月

(September 8th - October 7th) 癸酉
Mood swings would afflict you this month, making it particularly challenging to your emotional state. This would indirectly affect your work so you should remain focused.

農曆九月

(October 8th - November 7th) 甲戌
You may be feeling that others are taking advantage of you and you're feeling unappreciated. Be more assertive and don't be afraid to ask for what is due to you.

農曆十月

(November 8th - December 6th) 乙亥
If you were born in winter, avoid any activities that are related to water as it may cause you injuries.

農曆十一月

(December 7th 2019 - January 5th 2020) 丙子
You may be susceptible to overspending so try not to go for shopping so much or buy things you don't really need. Manage your finances carefully and try to save up.

農曆十二月

(January 6th - February 3rd 2020) 丁丑
Consider letting your ideas be known this month to your friends as they would be more than willing to lend you an ear.

癸酉 Gui You Day

Overview

It will be a fast and furious year for those that are working as full-time employees or those who born in the summer. One is expected to have a tight and busy schedule ahead which might require one to travel to another country. This might demotivate you, but you should take this as an opportunity to further enrich yourself.

 ## Wealth

You must resist the temptations of spending your hard-earned cash over costly and deluxe things. These luxurious belongings will only provide you with short-term happiness after spending big amount of money. As one is able to handle one's own finance well, one will smoothen one's wealth fortune approaching the end of the year.

 ## Relationships

Couples will be going through a tempestuous and shaky year of emotion. In order to be devoted into a long term relationship, coupled individuals must be frank to each other. That being said, think long and hard about the required process and effort to fix your relationship. Take charge of your own emotion and endeavour to compromise for better communication.

 ## Health

As the saying goes, "An ounce of prevention is worth a pound of cure", one should plan for frequent medical check-ups at least twice a year to avoid health issues such as high cholesterol level. Food and skin allergies might give you some tough time too. Having said that, try to find the balance between work and leisure time to prevent yourself from getting too stressed which will negatively affect your health.

Career

Brace yourself to encounter various hurdles in your career. Perseverance and persistence are your best friends to overcome these problems and to edge closer towards your goals. Treat the troubles as chances to build your character.

農曆正月

(February 4th - March 5th) 丙寅
In order to accomplish your targets more efficiently, you are advised to dive yourself into building team spirit as the team will provide you timely assistance at work.

農曆二月

(March 6th - April 4th) 丁卯
It is the time when you should utilize the great networking and communication skill of yours to gain help and connections while progressing towards your goals. You might even draw the assistance from Noble People as a result.

農曆三月

(April 5th - May 5th) 戊辰
Procrastination and laziness are your worst enemies while executing your arrangements. One shall always brace oneself and stick to one's plans.

農曆四月

(May 6th - June 5th) 己巳
Your discipline and personal virtues are keys to overcome the upcoming financial issues this month.

農曆五月

(June 6th - July 6th) 庚午
Those born in the summer may encounter strong sense of jealousy over the others this month. Get rid of it by being optimistic and hardworking to avoid any career distraction.

農曆六月

(July 7th - August 7th) 辛未
Your travel expenses will be filled by a great idea that can gain you significant income this month.

農曆七月

(August 8th - September 7th) 壬申
Those who work as full-time employees will particularly enjoy career advancement in the form of promotion and salary increment.

農曆八月

(September 8th - October 7th) 癸酉
Never let others persuade you to break the existing law at all costs and all times. Petty and unscrupulous people don't deserve your time and effort.

農曆九月

(October 8th - November 7th) 甲戌
You might experience the feeling of going unnoticed this month. Nevertheless, this is not the case in reality, thus do not take this to heart and focus more on the important matters in life.

農曆十月

(November 8th - December 6th) 乙亥
An auspicious turn of wealth fortune is in store for you! Besides, one will make the most of life's opportunities by grabbing them at the right time, especially if one was born in the autumn.

農曆十一月

(December 7th 2019 - January 5th 2020) 丙子
Serious food allergies may lead to severe health concerns. Therefore, be extra cautious of what you cannot eat to avoid unnecessary issues regarding your wellbeing. In other words, be more attentive of your diet.

農曆十二月

(January 6th - February 3rd 2020) 丁丑
Your opinions may differ from that of your partner more than usual this month. Having said that, it is advisable that you should try to avoid these disputes.

甲戌 Jia Xu Day

Overview

Individuals born in the autumn and winter seasons will experience lots of positivity in this year. Besides, the others shall be more careful around their peers as you are prone to upcoming rumours and sabotage. Do not be too kind to others especially those who don't appreciate your generosity. Take this year to analyse and determine your true friends.

 ## Wealth

Winter season babies shall come across wealth fortune. This can be seen in the form of various opportunities to work with people who acknowledge your contribution and effort. Nonetheless, as there will be fierce competition among all, you should contribute even more to outclass the others from taking over your position.

 ## Relationships

Both married and unmarried couples will be faced with insecurity and suspicion in this year. One shall not be too repulsive and ignorant over these issues as your partner may lose his or her confidence and patience over you. Instead, look for problem source and design an appropriate solution to deal with it to ensure better relationship with your partner.

 ## Health

Those who were born in autumn seasons must look after your stomach and digestive system more this year. The others shall come across health issues such as headaches and migraines due to bad stress management. In addition, one shall achieve the equilibrium between mental and physical health.

 ## Career

Your creativity and innovative ideas are your tools for good impressions for superiors though this may draw jealousy from the others. That being said, proceed carefully at work as your unscrupulous colleagues may try to replace you at your position and spread rumours. Never let these to be obstacles and learn to defend yourself when it matters.

農曆正月

(February 4th - March 5th) 丙寅
Assistance from colleagues and your excellent networking skills will be favoured with grand rewards.

農曆二月

(March 6th - April 4th) 丁卯
Workplace changes are in sight for you as you will have a new superior. Remember to leave a good impression to have a head-start in building professional relationship.

農曆三月

(April 5th - May 5th) 戊辰
Temptations such as buying luxurious things or parties may seem to be worthy, but these may require you to spend your hard-earned cash for short-term happiness. Therefore, think as you act.

農曆四月

(May 6th - June 5th) 己巳
Petty individuals may look for opportunities to sabotage and backstab you at work. That being said, be alert of the people that you befriend and entrusted with. Avoiding unscrupulous individuals will give you a rather smooth-sailing month ahead.

農曆五月

(June 6th - July 6th) 庚午
Those born during spring seasons will enjoy a rather good luck as they will be blessed with help from the others. Embrace the assistance and fully utilize them.

農曆六月

(July 7th - August 7th) 辛未
Greater and fiercer competition at workplace are in store for you as the competitors will step up their game and try to steal your acknowledgement away. Show your decent yet strong personality by holding firm to your thoughts and belief.

農曆七月

(August 8th - September 7th) 壬申
Both married and unmarried woman may be annoyed by problems regarding relationship as they feel as if they are underappreciated or went unnoticed.

農曆八月

(September 8th - October 7th) 癸酉
Several expenses may overwhelm you for this month. Drinking excessive beers will not subside the stress that you have. Instead, you should watch where your money goes to survive the month.

農曆九月

(October 8th - November 7th) 甲戌
Trust your instincts more. The right decisions usually are made in a calm and alert manner. Do not make decisions hastily.

農曆十月

(November 8th - December 6th) 乙亥
Those who were born in spring and winter season should brace themselves for several health issues this month. Thus, individuals should be more alert and take care of themselves well to resist the negative effects

農曆十一月

(December 7th 2019 - January 5th 2020) 丙子
A roller coaster ride is the best way to describe your emotion flow this month. Try to execute more control to handle the highs and lows of emotion in life. You are advised to head south while travelling.

農曆十二月

(January 6th - February 3rd 2020) 丁丑
Female individuals that are in relationship may encounter third party intrusion. Be careful of the ulterior intentions of these petty persons.

乙亥 **Yi Hai Day**

乙 *Yi*

亥 *Hai*

Overview

Overall, this year is looking to be mediocre for you. It can be more than what it is if you put in the effort to improve it. Perhaps you can review your work process or do some strategic execution to better equip yourself for progress and change, especially if you're in the creative field. By having an open mind, you would be able to achieve greater results at work.

 ## Wealth

When it comes to investments this year, go for long-term over short-term. Short-term investments might seem to produce quick results but, in this case, it will not be a favourable one. Any financial decisions you make this year should be treated carefully and with proper planning. Any uncertain factors that are not accounted for will hurt you in the long run. Consider the bigger picture.

 ## Relationships

For single men, there's a good possibility that they'll find the right partner this year. For single women on the other hand, they won't be experiencing such fortune. For them, it's better to focus on other aspects of their life for the time being. For those who are married, betrayal might happen.

 ## Health

In general, you would have good health this year. Still, you need to be on your toes while travelling as you may be susceptible to feet and head injuries. Gastric problems could also be a problem throughout the year. Fortunately, none of these are anything serious and your health is still good with all things considered; though it wouldn't hurt to take preventive measures.

 ## Career

Career opportunities are in abundance for you this year. Be assertive and take the opportunity enthusiastically instead of waiting and expecting it to come to you. Before taking any actions, do research your plan carefully beforehand. Proper work and a standard operation of procedures would propel you forward.

農曆正月

(February 4th - March 5th) 丙寅
You might get into an accident on the road this month so drive carefully.

農曆二月

(March 6th - April 4th) 丁卯
Your efforts at work will pay off this month and you may receive well-earned financial gains.

農曆三月

(April 5th - May 5th) 戊辰
If you let your emotions do all your thinking and decision making, you might live to regret it later on so have it check this month.

農曆四月

(May 6th - June 5th) 己巳
The circumstances might be unfavourable for you this month. To get through these troubling period, look for those close to you whom you can trust for advice and support. Be open to what they have to say and see if you can implement it.

農曆五月

(June 6th - July 6th) 庚午
Trouble might appear from your workplace this month as there are those who seek to turn the table against you. Make the necessary preparations.

農曆六月

(July 7th - August 7th) 辛未
When it comes to relationships this month, you and your partner will have some arguments. You may also have disagreements with your colleagues. Regardless, be diplomatic to every conflict in your life and make sure it ends amicably.

農曆七月

(August 8th - September 7th) 壬申
Your emotions shouldn't be allowed to take full control of your being. If you let strong negative emotions run its course, it might lead to regrettable outcomes. For any decision you're making, do it base on reality, facts and logic.

農曆八月

(September 8th - October 7th) 癸酉
This month, it would be favourable for you to travel south. Decisions that are decided firmly would have riveting results.

農曆九月

(October 8th - November 7th) 甲戌
Some people at work might seek to bring you down through petty gossip. Even if it's entirely baseless, don't let it get to you so much, ignore them and focus on your own goals instead.

農曆十月

(November 8th - December 6th) 乙亥
Extra work is to be expected of you this month as it is required for tangible results to happen. Stay determine and accept this with an open heart. Whatever work you put in will eventually earn you a proportionate reward in the end.

農曆十一月

(December 7th 2019 - January 5th 2020) 丙子
When it comes to legal documents this month, take your time to properly examine the papers. Acting hastily might have you end up taking responsibilities that would not benefit you.

農曆十二月

(January 6th - February 3rd 2020) 丁丑
You should pay attention to your health this month as potential issues might occur. Take preventive measures by going medical check ups to find any unseen symptoms. Particularly, you should be wary about your heart and eyes.

丙子 Bing Zi Day

Bing

Zi

Overview

For those who were born in spring, expect to have a prosperous year. Financially and intellectually, it's looking to be a good year for both aspects. Opportunities to expand your knowledge is abound and this growth will provide you new perspectives of your environment. Take advantage of this year by picking up new skills, and/or learning new things to further enhance your personal value.

Wealth

During the beginning of the year, you might feel like you're not financially secure. However, this is only temporary as you will only improve from there on. This is achievable through creative applications of your skills that you may accumulate wealth in unexpected ways. At the same time, make sure to implement your plans with careful thought and strategic thinking to make sure you're getting the most out of your opportunities.

Relationships

For women who are still single, this year you will have better opportunity to meet someone special. But, these opportunities can only happen if you allow them to. It is up to you to go out and put yourself in the position where you can meet new people. As for single men, you're likely to find someone; introduced to you by your mother.

Health

There's a chance your kidneys and bladders to be problematic this year with unhealthy eating habit being the culprit. Consider going on a diet or refraining from the less healthy options from your daily menu. If you were to be more mindful of what you eat, this would have a noticeable positive impact on your health in general.

Career

As this is the year with plenty of opportunities to grow intellectually, make the best out of it. For every opportunity that you take with an open heart will lead you to even more opportunities. You might even get a recommendation by your superiors to go on training or further studies which would bring your skillset to the next level; providing you a competitive edge.

農曆正月

(February 4th - March 5th) 丙寅
Be on a lookout this month for the many opportunities to increase your financial standing. Make sure you are ready to receive them as they appear.

農曆二月

(March 6th - April 4th) 丁卯
For married men, your significant other will be more demanding. As you try to balance your career and your love life, you will find this month to be difficult and tiring.

農曆三月

(April 5th - May 5th) 戊辰
In order for your work to progress, you need to be determined and apply some strategy to deal with it. Don't let yourself be involved in any unnecessary arguments and instead focus solely on your work.

農曆四月

(May 6th - June 5th) 己巳
If you consider to do any legal paperwork this month, especially if it's related to property or land, don't. Do it on another month as it would be more auspicious and provide better results.

農曆五月

(June 6th - July 6th) 庚午
Wealth opportunities are plenty so get ready for them. Make sure you're in the right capacity when they're given to you; otherwise it would be wasted.

農曆六月

(July 7th - August 7th) 辛未
If you were born during autumn or winter, this month may seem to be confusing and uncertain to you. It would be advisable for you to gather your thoughts and try to see things as they truly are instead of what they're perceived to be.

農曆七月

(August 8th - September 7th) 壬申
This month, your rivals seek to undermine you. They will do whatever it takes to bring you down but as long as you pay no mind to them, their actions would be for naught.

農曆八月

(September 8th - October 7th) 癸酉
Chances are, the biggest of your troubles this month is related to family; particularly related to your mother. Don't be confrontational about it, instead try to practice understanding and diplomacy.

農曆九月

(October 8th - November 7th) 甲戌
This month, you may be assigned with a new project or task. This is exactly a chance for you to prove your worth and display what value you bring to the table.

農曆十月

(November 8th - December 6th) 乙亥
If you were born during autumn or winter, this month you might find yourself travelling south.

農曆十一月
(December 7th 2019 - January 5th 2020) 丙子
Your rivals may grow stronger this month, but don't let them take your focus away from accomplishing your goals.

農曆十二月

(January 6th - February 3rd 2020) 丁丑
Your effort in working hard is finally paying off as you might receive some income from side projects. This is the proof that your hard work is fruitful.

丁丑 Ding Chou Day

Overview

In terms of career progression, a bountiful year awaits you as you will be met with many opportunities that would help you in realising your goals. If there is a bigger and more illustrious company that you've always had your eyes on, there's a good chance you may get to work there.

 ## Wealth

For the first half of the year, you will be able to gain a significant amount of fortune. While this boon is merely temporary, true wealth would be yours if you put your back in it. With effort, it will lead to power, authority and reputation. Being diligent will allow you to reap the benefits.

 ## Relationships

For those who are single, you might be able to meet someone who is your type. For attached individuals however, they may find themselves in argument with their partners that could escalate to be constant and unhealthy to the relationship. Thus, try to minimise the problem early on.

 ## Health

By taking good care of your wellbeing, you're likely to be in a good condition this year. Take note of what you eat as you may be susceptible to digestive disorders and minor issues like food poisoning by the year's end. This is especially so if you were born in winter.

 ## Career

Now is the time for you to take your position to a whole new level. A higher position requires responsibility, as such try to present your superiors with fresh ideas pertaining leadership skills. There may be a chance for better job opportunities as others will take notice of what you have to offer.

農曆正月

(February 4th - March 5th) 丙寅
In this month, your financial luck is looking strong; possibly due to clever ideas that you came up with and capitalised thus far.

農曆二月

(March 6th - April 4th) 丁卯
As you will continue to enjoy favourable wealth luck, make the best of this window of opportunity to negotiate as many positive deals as possible.

農曆三月

(April 5th - May 5th) 戊辰
Try to get friendly with your superior and build a sturdy relationship with them as you can count on them for support for future ideas and work.

農曆四月

(May 6th - June 5th) 己巳
Procrastinations and distractions will be prevalent this month but pay them no heed as it will not do you any good.

農曆五月

(June 6th - July 6th) 庚午
Career-wise, there is a chance for advancement in the form of either a promotion or a job offer at a different workplace.

農曆六月

(July 7th - August 7th) 辛未
Around this part of the year, you may feel like you're open to try new things. Take the opportunity to work on a fresh skill or discover your talents.

農曆七月

(August 8th - September 7th) 壬申
Due to work, you may have to travel frequently this month. Your spouse might find this to be a problem if you're married.

農曆八月

(September 8th - October 7th) 癸酉
Ignore petty rumours that might crop up this month and focus on what is important. As long as you have your priorities straight, you'll be fine.

農曆九月

(October 8th - November 7th) 甲戌
For this month, you will find yourself to have a surplus of positive energy that you are able to utilise it in order to do quality work. Just make sure you don't step on your superiors' toes.

農曆十月

(November 8th - December 6th) 乙亥
This month, you might be approached with a partnership offer. However, do not agree to this immediately as the timing isn't good. Decide about the partnership on a later date.

農曆十一月

(December 7th 2019 - January 5th 2020) 丙子
There's a chance that your ideas might get stolen by some people who will claim it to be theirs. Make sure to cover your ground and at the same time choose who you share information with carefully.

農曆十二月

(January 6th - February 3rd 2020) 丁丑
Your busy work schedule might have taken a toll on your health and as such you may be suffering from stress-related health issues. Give yourself a break and go for a holiday to catch your breath.

戊寅 Wu Yin Day

Wu

Yin

Overview
This is a year to look forward to as it would be auspicious. If you have invested in real estate, expect your wealth to increase. There's also a possibility for you to be in a new home or acquire a new property. It's a very good year for you in terms of wealth and you will have the opportunity to further its growth and make the best out of your investments.

 ## Wealth
This is a very good year for you in terms of wealth. Take advantage of this and utilise every opportunity that comes your way wisely. It's advisable for you to take your time to form a solid base for your investments and finances to ensure continuous prosperity well into the future, allowing you to generate more income.

 ## Relationships
It will be a rewarding year for single men when it comes to romance as there's a possibility to meet the right partner. For those who are already in a marriage, there might be some problems. Before they spiral out of control, settle them quickly. For single women, the best time for romance would be when autumn comes around.

 ## Health
When it comes to health, this year you would be particularly affected emotionally. Whatever negative feeling you have can be remedied through meditation or relaxing activities to ensure the clarity of mind. Self-reflection would also be beneficial. If you are older than forty years old, go for check-ups for your heart.

 ## Career
In terms of career, your prospects are quite bright. This is only the case if you collaborate with other people. Form lasting relationships with your colleagues so that the help you get from them will be enough to overcome any challenges that comes your way. Other people can offer you many forms of support.

農曆正月

(February 4th - March 5th) 丙寅
Be more assertive by taking every opportunity that you see, start new opportunities and develop innovative ideas.

農曆二月

(March 6th - April 4th) 丁卯
You have the chance to create some side income this month and you may get the idea on how to do so from your friends.

農曆三月

(April 5th - May 5th) 戊辰
Your leg might be susceptible to injuries this month, especially around your knees and ankles. Be wary with any activity that might compromise them such as exercising or sports.

農曆四月

(May 6th - June 5th) 己巳
Your health might cause you to spend money this month. This can be prevented if you are mindful of any sharp objects in your vicinity that might cause you harm.

農曆五月

(June 6th - July 6th) 庚午
If you have been employed for a while and thinking you deserve more benefits or even a raise, now's a good month to ask for them.

農曆六月

(July 7th - August 7th) 辛未
Be careful with your words this month as it may be offensive to certain people. If you are unsure if something would be offensive, simply not speak.

農曆七月

(August 8th - September 7th) 壬申
You might be thinking too much over things you have no control over, but it would only hold you back from moving forward and being productive.

農曆八月

(September 8th - October 7th) 癸酉
This month, you might be facing some trouble at home that could affect your work so handle it wisely before it gets worse.

農曆九月

(October 8th - November 7th) 甲戌
There may be people out to steal your ideas this month so be careful with who you choose to confide them to.

農曆十月

(November 8th - December 6th) 乙亥
Keep your emotions in check especially when it comes to making decisions as you might regret it if you let your emotions decide for you.

農曆十一月

(December 7th 2019 - January 5th 2020) 丙子
Take a break this month to get away from work-related stress.

農曆十二月

(January 6th - February 3rd 2020) 丁丑
For any problem that appears this month, handle them immediately. If you let these problems fester, you might be facing worse long-term effects.

己卯 **Ji Mao Day**

Overview

There will be plenty of opportunities relating to your career this year that you can work on. It might even lead to travelling for work or a form of promotion. As such, it would be favourable for you to be more proactive to take advantage of these opportunities. Your personal life however would be plagued by ambiguity and confusion. It would be up to you to actively seek out the answers to your questions.

 ## Wealth

If you have been planning to travel or go for a vacation for a while now, you will finally be able to do so. When you travel, you will gain new experience that can expand your perspective as well as forming new connections with people who may help you grow as a person. It's an ideal year to make personal improvements and learn more about yourself.

 ## Relationships

For those who are in a long-term relationship and planning to settle down, this would be an auspicious year for you. Be honest with what you expect of one another and discuss your plans properly as it would be beneficial. A clear two-way communication should be established early on so that you may take your relationship to the next level without much difficulty.

 ## Health

Stomach and blood related problems are something you should be looking out for as they can be rather disruptive of your daily routine. These problems may manifest itself in the form of food poisoning or indigestion. Seek medical attention as soon as the symptoms appear so that the negative effects can be minimized.

 ## Career

This year, you can expect good things from your workplace as you may be getting some form of career advancement. You might be excited over this prospect, but don't let your overall health be neglected due to your work. Every aspect of your life is important in their own way and you need to balance them all with wisdom.

農曆正月
(February 4th - March 5th) 丙寅
Your hard work will be acknowledged this month and rewards in the form of wealth would be gained. Keep up the momentum and maintain your professionalism.

農曆二月
(March 6th - April 4th) 丁卯
This month, your wealth luck continues. Continue with the pace you're going to make the most out of this opportunity. For men, you will enjoy better luck this month if you're looking for a romantic partner.

農曆三月
(April 5th - May 5th) 戊辰
It's a good month for love and romance this month for women. To enjoy more opportunities, you need to reconsider your expectations and standards in such a way where you're more openminded. You might find a pleasant surprise should you give yourself the chance to be.

農曆四月
(May 6th - June 5th) 己巳
Stress would permeate throughout this month as a result from relationship problems. Give yourself a break and look at the situation carefully to see if you can find a realistic way to resolve the conflict. Don't drag trouble to other aspects of your life.

農曆五月
(June 6th - July 6th) 庚午
It will be an inspirational month for you as you would be able to come up with fresh new ideas easily. You may even be able to generate more income out of these ideas if you put in the effort to bring it into reality.

農曆六月
(July 7th - August 7th) 辛未
It can be expected of you to go around travelling here and there this month. Travelling itself would do you good, but you need to be vigilant around food. You might get food poisoning if you don't practice good hygiene so try to be careful with what you eat.

農曆七月
(August 8th - September 7th) 壬申
Your mind is in a volatile state this month as your emotions are unstable. Try your best to keep your anger to yourself and not lash out to other people. Otherwise, they might be negatively affected by your temper and in turn make things worse for everyone.

農曆八月
(September 8th - October 7th) 癸酉
Even if you're the leader of your group, you are not obliged to help anyone in solving their own problem. You should allow yourself to distance yourself from their trouble instead of actively trying to help them.

農曆九月
(October 8th - November 7th) 甲戌
Problems at home might be expected for married couples this month. The conflict can be minimized through a diplomatic approach in dealing with the differences and disagreements with patience and understanding.

農曆十月
(November 8th - December 6th) 乙亥
Competition is brewing at your work place this month and you will need to put in extra effort if you don't wish to be left behind.

農曆十一月
(December 7th 2019 - January 5th 2020) 丙子
Competition continues to strive at your workplace this month. The pressure from working harder might push you to a breaking point, but you shouldn't do anything counterproductive. Shortcuts and any ethically questionable behaviour should be avoided. This whole experience would be a valuable lesson for you.

農曆十二月
(January 6th - February 3rd 2020) 丁丑
Just because you've been hard at work doesn't mean you should be neglecting your relationships. Put aside some time to spend with your loved ones. You could try doing a new activity together as the experience would strengthen your bonds.

庚辰 **Geng Chen Day**

Geng

Chen

Overview

You will experience boredom as the first few months of this year may be dull and mediocre for you and this may remain the same for some time. One should design certain detailed and genuine plans in order to change this situation. You may be a little more stressed and tired than usual, but remember, you will see the rainbow after the storm.

 ## Wealth

As the saying goes, "Go confidently in the direction of your dreams, live the life you have imagined", one should pursue one's dreams and goals without any fear. A way to edge closer towards your destination would be to adopt a proactive approach. Moreover, spend time and effort to improve your service and product services to meet the market's trends and demands. One would accomplish great things if one does his best.

 ## Relationships

In the first half of the year, your chance of being in a romantic relationship would be slim. Nevertheless, relationship fortune will change approaching the second half year. Having said that, one should dedicate one's effort to focus more on other areas such as career since this is not a great romance year for you. Remember, true love usually appears when you are not looking for it.

 ## Health

The health of your kidney, eyes and heart will be your primary concern this year, especially during autumn and winter seasons. Look after yourself more such as to consult doctor immediately when you're ill in order to overcome health issues.

 ## Career

Slow work growth that may lead to frustration and fatigue are your enemies at workplace this year. However, this shouldn't restrain you from spending effort and focus to your job since the lesser you work the lesser you achieve. Besides, this is also a time when you should utilize it on gaining new skills or knowledge to further enrich your capabilities. Increased personal values and better opportunities in the future will be in store for you as a result.

農曆正月

(February 4th - March 5th) 丙寅
Partnerships and human networks are keys to a successful life. Those who born in the winter will enjoy these complementing relationships and collaboration this month.

農曆二月

(March 6th - April 4th) 丁卯
Incoming pregnancy health risks will be in sight for prospective mothers this month. Stay attentive and take care.

農曆三月

(April 5th - May 5th) 戊辰
Remain active and keep your energy at a reasonable high level to avoid procrastination. You may want to restructure your resolutions to keep a fresh mind and gradual momentum.

農曆四月

(May 6th - June 5th) 己巳
You're bothered by a weakened mentality due to fatigue. However, things may take an even inauspicious turn this month, causing higher stress level in you. You may want to look after yourself more to promote equal good health to both mental and physical.

農曆五月

(June 6th - July 6th) 庚午
Allocate some focus to watch over your spouse on health concerns as they might not be aware of the problems. If the issue persists, you may want to intervene and seek solutions for it on behalf of them.

農曆六月

(July 7th - August 7th) 辛未
Obey the rules at all costs and all times. Avoid going too far when it comes to executing your jobs. Also, practice your ethics and honesty at work.

農曆七月

(August 8th - September 7th) 壬申
Upcoming health concerns especially to the digestive system will be in store for those who born in autumn and winter seasons. Watch out on what you eat.

農曆八月

(September 8th - October 7th) 癸酉
There are rivals that will seek ways such as spreading rumours in order to replace you at your position. One will need to be attentive and cautious all the time to face the fierce competitions among colleagues.

農曆九月

(October 8th - November 7th) 甲戌
You will probably be more pessimistic and negative in this period of time. Talk it out with you loved ones, ask for their advices and help. Your worries will be subsided eventually.

農曆十月

(November 8th - December 6th) 乙亥
You should keep a close eye on your diet as there are potential wellbeing risks regarding your stomach this month. Plan as you eat since problems such as stomach flu or food poisoning may be lurking around if one doesn't take care of his stomach well.

農曆十一月

(December 7th 2019 - January 5th 2020) 丙子
Practice team spirit with your colleagues to build better network and teamwork. Their genuine assistance and support are keys to solve issues with your superiors.

農曆十二月

(January 6th - February 3rd 2020) 丁丑
One should separate business from pleasure as one shall keep one's domestic problems away from the office. Learn to set borders between those two, do not let any of them intervene the other.

辛巳 Xin Si Day

Overview

This year, expect additional workload coming your way. With that in mind, manage your responsibilities with wisdom so that you may hone your professional aspect. In-between juggling your tasks, set some time for yourself to recover as to maintain your flow. When you work hard, you may also set yourself to be a target of jealous eyes. Even so, stand by your principle so that you remain true to your causes. Practice kindness and be more open and you will find these values to be rewarding.

 ## Wealth

Wealth prospects is looking good for you this year. Still, it's not an excuse for you to go crazy with your finances. Plan your budget strategically and try not to give in to impulsive spending. Exercise self-discipline to avoid overspending and future problems that comes with it.

 ## Relationships

When it comes to disagreements, choose your words wisely and go for diplomacy and compromises whenever possible. If you don't think before you speak, you may unintentionally offend others. For married women, their marriage might demand more of their time. For single men, they'll have to get themselves out there if they're looking for someone special.

 ## Health

Your health outlook for this year is rather positive in general. That being said, there are possibilities for minor injuries such as sprains that could stem from performing chores or exercising. It can potentially worsen to something more severe if not properly treated early on. Regular health check-up is recommended as your heart is at risk of some strain as well.

Career

Somewhere during the middle of the year, there might be a job offer waiting for you. Until then, maintain amicable relationships with your current workplace as you shouldn't make any hasty decision. Whatever plans you might have, it's always good to maintain good relationships with your bosses and keep working hard as they might assist you in the future as your referrals.

農曆正月

(February 4th - March 5th) 丙寅
Expect competition this month at your workplace. Make the necessary preparations and strategies to gain a competitive edge. You're also susceptible to shoulder injuries so be careful with them.

農曆二月

(March 6th - April 4th) 丁卯
This month, you may feel like your superior is being unfair in favouring other colleagues. Don't take this personally as what value you bring to your team is not equal to everyone else.

農曆三月

(April 5th - May 5th) 戊辰
The opportunity to travel might present itself this month so make preparations for travelling. At the same time, try not to procrastinate and avoid becoming lazy.

農曆四月

(May 6th - June 5th) 己巳
This month will reward you financially through good teamwork. It's a good time to work with other people and flexing your social skills.

農曆五月

(June 6th - July 6th) 庚午
A job offer is most likely in the bag for you this month. Before taking it up, think it through carefully and weight out the options you have.

農曆六月

(July 7th - August 7th) 辛未
For men, their personal and professional lives have a tendency to be mixed together. Try to separate these two aspects of your life so that they won't bring complications to each other.

農曆七月

(August 8th - September 7th) 壬申
As far as driving is concerned, you may run into some trouble with the law this month. Make sure you have yourself covered in appropriately so that there won't be anything against you.

農曆八月

(September 8th - October 7th) 癸酉
You might feel low this month. Alcohol may seem like a good idea to you but avoid the temptation as it won't solve any problem.

農曆九月

(October 8th - November 7th) 甲戌
This month, don't be afraid to let your creativity loose. Try out new things, come up with new ideas and give refreshing new spin to old concepts.

農曆十月

(November 8th - December 6th) 乙亥
You might be travelling again this month. A change in scenery is always refreshing and any new experience adds to your knowledge.

農曆十一月

(December 7th 2019 - January 5th 2020) 丙子
Expect domestic problems this month. Whenever they appear, handle it as soon as possible in order for them not to affect other parts of your life.

農曆十二月

(January 6th - February 3rd 2020) 丁丑
This month, stay true to your ethics, honesty and the rules as you may find yourself in questionable situations. It would be your own fault if you allow it to happen.

壬午 **Ren Wu Day**

Ren

Wu

Overview

When you are uncertain or find yourself in stagnation, your way our is through the help of others. Through good team management, you will be able to find recognition and achieve your goals. Strengthen your relationships with others and make sure your social network has extensive reach. Be more adaptable to whatever comes and keep an open mind.

 ## Wealth

Overall, this year your wealth luck is looking good. However, it does require work on your part to utilise it. Traveling would be one way to go about it though it does need prior research and planning. On anything related to investment, you need to be very careful about it. Make sure your expenses and budget are kept in check and dabble into investment only once you're financially secured.

 ## Relationships

The person you have your eyes on may give their attention to someone else, causing you to feel intense jealousy this year. Don't be too hung up on this as everyone will find the right person for them eventually. If you are already in a marriage, make sure that your relationship is not jeopardised by unfounded rumours or influences from your friends.

 ## Health

For those who are forty years old or more, pay attention to the amount of sugar you consume as well as your cholesterol levels. It's better to take preventative measures before things get serious. Perhaps go for a full medical check-up from time to time and do what you can to take care of your health.

 ## Career

Your time for career progression will come eventually but you must be patient about it. If you are involved in sales or work that requires travelling, it will be a productive year for you. You may be faced with some competition but if you play your cards right, these rivals might be turned into allies.

農曆正月

(February 4th - March 5th) 丙寅
Put your ego aside and realise that there are others who have better ideas when it comes to projects at work. Despite so, give your best support nonetheless.

農曆二月

(March 6th - April 4th) 丁卯
Changing jobs might be something you're considering but remember to decide on this matter based on facts and current situation rather than relying on your emotions.

農曆三月

(April 5th - May 5th) 戊辰
This month, work hard and be assertive at your work place. Make the best out of every opportunity you have to shine.

農曆四月

(May 6th - June 5th) 己巳
Consider what your priorities really are and exercise some self-reflection on your style of work. A change of your modus operandi might allow you to achieve your goals better.

農曆五月

(June 6th - July 6th) 庚午
Refrain from spontaneous behaviours and plan every future action well. By doing so, you will be maximizing the favourable results of these activity.

農曆六月

(July 7th - August 7th) 辛未
Your words or action may seem harmless to you, but it may cause unintentional offence. Keep in mind how you carry and project yourself to others.

農曆七月

(August 8th - September 7th) 壬申
This month, your wealth luck is improving. For men who are still looking for potential partners, it's a good month to do so.

農曆八月

(September 8th - October 7th) 癸酉
All your efforts will eventually bear fruit this month. With the results in your sight, use it as motivation to continue with your hard work.

農曆九月

(October 8th - November 7th) 甲戌
You may be starting a new relationship this month. For women in particular, they may need to keep quiet about this new relationship.

農曆十月

(November 8th - December 6th) 乙亥
While your wealth luck is improving, your health may be susceptible to problems. In the pursuit of wealth, do take better care of your own body.

農曆十一月

(December 7th 2019 - January 5th 2020) 丙子
You might be feeling angry or suspicious towards your partner but don't act on your emotions. Learn to compromise and approach your problems with practical and amiable solutions.

農曆十二月

(January 6th - February 3rd 2020) 丁丑
Doubt might cloud your mind this month and you will find it difficult to make any decision. If need be, rely on your friends to help you realise what is the right thing to do.

癸未 Gui Wei Day

Overview

If you wish to advance your career this year, partnerships and collaborations will be the way. Build up a network of individuals who are beneficial to you by having a diverse set of skills and talent at your disposal. Through their help, your workload will be reduced and pooling your ideas together will innovate your outlook. Have an open mind when it comes to what others can offer you so that you may utilise your resources well.

 ## Wealth

This year, money won't come easy to you. In order for you to stay ahead of the curve, you need to be creative in reinventing the way you go about things in order to be more efficient in your work. By discussing with others, solutions are easier to achieve so do not hesitate in getting the aid of others to improve your financial standing.

 ## Relationships

Through your network of friends, you might be able to find your ideal partner. If you are already in a relationship, some problems may occur in the form of third party influence or betrayal. Make sure you have an honest two-way communication with your partner and be on a look out for anything that might compromise your relationship.

 ## Health

If you are still young, your health won't be causing you much issue. For older folks however, their blood sugar level might be at risk. Unforeseen health issues can be avoided should you take preventive steps such as abstaining or at least moderate your sugar and cholesterol intake.

Career

Rivalry at your workplace will make you more susceptible to stress. You should find allies that you are able to trust and rely on to lighten your load and defend your reputation should the need occurs. Being a loner won't be favourable for you as there is strength in number. Work to improve your social skills so that others may come to your aid whenever you need them.

農曆正月
(February 4th - March 5th) 丙寅
There's an air of jealousy at work this month as there are people who feel like your superior favours you over them. Regardless of how these petty people perceive you, ultimately, they don't matter in the bigger picture and you shouldn't let yourself be affected by what they think or say. What matters is the work that you deliver.

農曆二月
(March 6th - April 4th) 丁卯
This month, let your ideas flourish by sharing it with others. Have confidence in what you come up with as it will be well-received and beneficial for your work in the future.

農曆三月
(April 5th - May 5th) 戊辰
Trouble is brewing at work as you find yourself in disagreements with your colleagues. These problems can be resolved diplomatically through compromise and empathy. They should be settled as soon as possible before it grows into something worse.

農曆四月
(May 6th - June 5th) 己巳
You may expect a financial boon this month for the efforts you have invested in a side project. By working hard, you will see the fruits of your labour soon enough.

農曆五月
(June 6th - July 6th) 庚午
It will be a busy month for you which can contribute to an increase in your stress level. This in turn may manifest itself as poor physical health. The symptoms of stress and illness can be lessened or avoided altogether should you alleviate the root cause of the problem that is stress. Take some time to relax.

農曆六月
(July 7th - August 7th) 辛未
You may offend the people around you unknowingly with your words and actions if you're not careful with them. Be more sensitive to others and how they react to you.

農曆七月
(August 8th - September 7th) 壬申
An increase in financial luck is to be expected this month along with financial gains. This is particularly true if you were born in summer season.

農曆八月
(September 8th - October 7th) 癸酉
Through business travels, you would be able to find new opportunities. It can only be beneficial for you should you make yourself aware of these.

農曆九月
(October 8th - November 7th) 甲戌
You might be feeling unsatisfied and tired this month and not being content with how things are. Rather than waiting for this spell of ennui to disappear eventually, try to find out what made you feel this way. At the same time, don't do anything that would aggravate the matter.

農曆十月
(November 8th - December 6th) 乙亥
There will be a lot of distractions all around you that are mostly trivial in nature. You should remain focus on your goals and the things that matter. Keep a distance from everything else so your vision can remain clear.

農曆十一月
(December 7th 2019 - January 5th 2020) 丙子
This month, it will be rewarding for your career should you travel south. It will bring more opportunities that can be translated into more gains.

農曆十二月
(January 6th - February 3rd 2020) 丁丑
Your colleagues might be able to share very useful information to you that you can utilise for your own benefit. It may not seem to be applicable now, but you might find it handy when you're undertaking a new project in the future.

甲申 Jia Shen Day

Overview
The presence of uncertainties will cause a chaotic year ahead. You shall not expect a smooth year as this brings even more stress when problems occur. Having said that, you should keep a low profile and focus on next year's arrangements and proceed with caution this year. While tough times are incoming, you must learn to be more capable by acquiring new skillsets and explore fresh things in life.

Wealth
Embrace the travel openings with opened arms since they will fruit excellent returns and fresh experience to enhance your personal values. Individuals that are in relationship should have a close watch on their bank accounts to avoid any misunderstandings or issues.

Relationships
A tough year ahead for couples who are married as patience among each other will be questioned. Chances are break up is in store if individual cannot solve the quarrels. Never escalate things to raise misunderstandings between the two of you. Couples should work hand in hand to talk things over and fix the problems. Also, take these hurdles as opportunities to strengthen your relationship. Furthermore, single men and women are in for a fruitless year of romance.

Health
If you thought medical check-ups are unnecessary, think again. As the saying goes, "Prevention works better than cure", individuals must tackle early signs of illness to have effective precautionary steps to prevent yourself from getting sick or injured.

Career
Work trips are coupled with possible financial openings this year. Stay attentive to the little things in life and be proactive enough to grab the opportunities as soon as you can. If the travel openings are not favouring you, it only means your work growth is rather slow this year.

農曆正月

(February 4th - March 5th) 丙寅
Excellent wealth fortune are in sight for those who were born during autumn seasons this month.

農曆二月

(March 6th - April 4th) 丁卯
An even auspicious turn of wealth fortune for you this month! Nonetheless, your prospects in other areas in life are less impressive.

農曆三月

(April 5th - May 5th) 戊辰
Several hurdles are set along your path to slow your progression of pursuing dreams. Instead of being annoyed by this, stay modest at all times as everyone has both good and bad days.

農曆四月

(May 6th - June 5th) 己巳
Uncertainties are lurking around your relationships, some might be in the form of betrayal. Married female individuals are particularly vulnerable to these issues.

農曆五月

(June 6th - July 6th) 庚午
Tension is building among colleagues at workplace this month. The opening to perform your best traits might lead into getting ahead of yourself. Therefore, act accordingly to whatever that will throw at you and stay humble.

農曆六月

(July 7th - August 7th) 辛未
Reposition your mentality and conform to both the good and bad days in life this month. There are disappointments around, thus it's best to be realistic and open-minded at all times.

農曆七月

(August 8th - September 7th) 壬申
Fortune is favouring you to look for a competent business or career partner. They will take over the role of fine middle man and trustable persons.

農曆八月

(September 8th - October 7th) 癸酉
An auspicious travelling month for you ahead! However, refrain from being overexcited or over-relaxed on the possible adventure. Be sure to have close watch on your health and safety namely taking care of your food intake as chances are you will have risk of stomach flu or food poisoning.

農曆九月

(October 8th - November 7th) 甲戌
Practice the caution on your individual documents and property this month as there are risk lurking around them.

農曆十月

(November 8th - December 6th) 乙亥
Autumn babies are graced with excellent fortune this month. Go ahead and proceed with your plans aggressively to pursue your goals as it is favouring you to claim good returns.

農曆十一月

(December 7th 2019 - January 5th 2020) 丙子
Practice your patience and caution while penning signature on real estate documents. Do not be overexcited as this will disrupt your decision. Rash choice will only fruit bad outcomes.

農曆十二月

(January 6th - February 3rd 2020) 丁丑
Auspicious travelling month for you since the events are favouring. Remember, be careful and watchful at all costs especially when you're in another country or state to obey the laws and traditions there.

乙酉 Yi You Day

Overview

The key to your success this year lies in the people in your social circle. If your colleagues have any ideas, take note of what they have to say. Make the most out of what your mentors have to offer be it actual assistance or knowledge. Make yourself valuable to the people around you by being helpful and kind. If you stay on this path, your social network will expand together with your good reputation; this will definitely open many doors in the future.

 ## Wealth

This year, you can increase your wealth by investing your money with other people and collaborations with others. Bear in mind that just because socialising is generally favourable for you doesn't mean you should spend too much money on it alone. Manage your finances well by spending it only where it matters and try to pick your acquaintances carefully.

 ## Relationships

In terms of love, your outlook for this year is average. For women in relationships, expect some competition with friends with ulterior motives. They may directly or indirectly affect your relationship. For men who are in a relationship, be mindful of what other people say about what you have with your current partner. It may cause damage and strain to your relationship if you take what they say to heart.

 ## Health

Stress is something you have to deal with this year as well as the headaches and migraines that comes with it. Take the necessary steps to mitigate these symptoms. Stomach related issues such as food poisoning and stomach ache might also afflict you so watch your diet. Solve the main cause of all of this directly by managing your stress levels well.

 ## Career

Your professional contacts will provide you with plenty of opportunities this year. At work, put in the necessary effort to gain acknowledgement and build up your reputation. At the same time, remain humble and give credit where credit is due to those who have helped you along the way. Disagreements and animosity at work can be avoided by having strong, healthy relationships with your colleagues.

農曆正月

(February 4th - March 5th) 丙寅
A great start to this year for you would be forging strong bonds with your business partners or colleagues. This will set the stage for any future opportunity that might come your way.

農曆二月

(March 6th - April 4th) 丁卯
Keep an open mind as those close to you might have some great ideas that you can utilise. Be sure to hear them out.

農曆三月

(April 5th - May 5th) 戊辰
You may run into some argument with your superior but try to be emphatic about the situation to avoid dissatisfaction and keep up the momentum you have with your work.

農曆四月

(May 6th - June 5th) 己巳
Those on the same level as you might like your ideas but it will take some convincing to get through to your superior. Plan your proposals and presentations carefully in order to persuade them.

農曆五月

(June 6th - July 6th) 庚午
Doing the same thing over and over again might not get you anywhere this month. Consider innovating with how you do your work.

農曆六月

(July 7th - August 7th) 辛未
Instead of squabbling with your colleagues, find a middle ground with them and come to a compromise. In the long term, this will be more beneficial than a ruined relationship with them.

農曆七月

(August 8th - September 7th) 壬申
Accidents that are minor in nature might occur if you are to travel within this month. Keep an eye out for your personal belongings and safety.

農曆八月

(September 8th - October 7th) 癸酉
It's a favourable month for wealth and this is particularly true if you were born in summer. There will be plenty of opportunities and take on them as much as possible.

農曆九月

(October 8th - November 7th) 甲戌
You may be feeling that your boss is unjustifiably pushing you around. Don't be a doormat and stand up for yourself. You may also opt to be diplomatic and resolve the situation through proper means.

農曆十月

(November 8th - December 6th) 乙亥
Decisions that carry a lot of weight have to wait as this is not a good time. You're not focused at the moment due to wild mood swings.

農曆十一月
(December 7th 2019 - January 5th 2020) 丙子
There will be those around you who may wish to borrow your money. If you wish to help them out, make sure that you're doing it within acceptable boundaries.

農曆十二月

(January 6th - February 3rd 2020) 丁丑
Women in relationships have to beware of any outside influence threatening your relationship this month. Examine any activities that seems dubious and questionable.

丙戌 **Bing Xu Day**

Overview

It's high time you take it slow and do some introspection. Look where you are at right now in your life and think carefully about what's ahead. With better self-awareness, you would realistically be able to make the most out of the options available. In terms of relationships, some issues may crop up this year and you should keep your emotions under control. For wealth related matters, property would provide better returns.

 Wealth

Overall, this year is average for you when it comes to your wealth luck. In fact, you might even lose some amount of money. Take care of your finances better and go for property investment instead. Having said that, take the effort to research before jumping in. If you go into investment blindly, you might be faced with legal problems which translates to more money lost.

 Relationships

There are a lot of opportunities to meet a romantic partner this year, provided you're a single woman yourself. At the same time, be clear with your intent in the pursue in romance so that you won't waste anyone's time. For married men, expect difficulties.

 Health

For those born in winter, take care of your immunity system. Fo everyone else, your health is looking good this year. Even so, it's best if you improve your health however you can whether through a healthier diet or exercising. Make sure these health-related improvements aren't such a drastic change that it can eventually become part of your daily ritual.

Career

If your work requires creativity, you're in luck as this year will provide you a boost in productivity and inspiration. You're also likely to be met with a promotion and opportunity to travel. Should you choose to travel, it will possibly open up the door to more opportunities.

農曆正月

(February 4th - March 5th) 丙寅
A month of inspiration will allow you to generate many good ideas that are well-received at your workplace. This in turn ensures an increase in wealth opportunities.

農曆二月

(March 6th - April 4th) 丁卯
If you have any side projects, they will prove to be fruitful this month as you have strong Indirect wealth luck in this month.

農曆三月

(April 5th - May 5th) 戊辰
Here's your chance to advance in your career as a promotion or other career advancement opportunities might be around the corner this month.

農曆四月

(May 6th - June 5th) 己巳
This month, you might find yourself to be travelling. If you do so, especially if you're going to a foreign country, read the fine print when it comes to the local law.

農曆五月

(June 6th - July 6th) 庚午
Take all the opportunities that you see coming your way as you're experiencing strong wealth luck this month.

農曆六月

(July 7th - August 7th) 辛未
This month, you might have to deal with certain problems. Whatever the problem may be, don't forget to think it through carefully before deciding on a plan of action.

農曆七月

(August 8th - September 7th) 壬申
Your workplace will likely be a competitive environment this month. It would be wise for you to make sure your interests are safeguarded and at the same time maintain amiable relationship with colleagues.

農曆八月

(September 8th - October 7th) 癸酉
Careful with what you share at work, as the ideas that you have might get stolen by colleagues who would present them as it was theirs.

農曆九月

(October 8th - November 7th) 甲戌
Your physical well-being requires attention this month so do try to exercise more and eat healthily.

農曆十月

(November 8th - December 6th) 乙亥
In this month, you have to be patient. Take your time with everything and try not to rush; especially if what you're rushing into is money-related.

農曆十一月

(December 7th 2019 - January 5th 2020) 丙子
Your workplace requires you to be as clear and honest as possible to avoid any misunderstand between you and your colleagues and bosses.

農曆十二月

(January 6th - February 3rd 2020) 丁丑
You need to be more proactive this month. If you were to take your time trying to make sure whatever it is you're working on to be perfect, you're only procrastinating. Just do it, don't think about it much.

 丁亥 **Ding Hai Day**

Overview

Careful not to breakdown from being overwhelmed as a busy and challenging year awaits you. While you focus on achieving your goals, always remember to catch your breath from time to time and take it easy. Rather than doing multiple tasks at the same time, consider taking them on one at a time while giving yourself ample time to recover.

 Wealth

Practice some caution when it comes to wealth as you're susceptible to financial losses this year. Make sure you keep your spending under control as to not incur significant financial damage. For the first half of the year, it's not so bad but by the time mid-year rolls around you will need to practice restrain.

 Relationships

For women in relationships, there's a good chance to finally tie the knot this year. For married women, however, this year will be rather difficult as they will find themselves with stress and emotional turmoil. Whenever there's an argument, try to settle it amicably so that whatever problem you're having wouldn't spiral out of control. For men, they should keep in mind that they shouldn't risk the relationship they have for something temporary.

 Health

You might consider taking care of your health better as minor health issues may appear this year; particularly towards the second half of the year. You should especially be mindful of this if you were born in autumn or winter. Practice healthy activities such as regular exercise and watching what you eat. Try to actively be on guard regarding your personal safety if ever you participate in water-related activities.

 Career

There's a chance that you'll be at odds with your superiors this year. Try to settle whatever arguments you're having diplomatically so that you won't fall out of your boss' good grace. Make sure you work on your communication skill and have good relationships with your colleagues to ensure that they'll have your back when it comes to work.

農曆正月

(February 4th - March 5th) 丙寅
Plenty of opportunities are here with the new year and you might even earn yourself a promotion. A good start for the year as you will have good wealth luck.

農曆二月

(March 6th - April 4th) 丁卯
This is the right time to make the best out of any opportunity that comes your way and earn yourself a considerable financial boon.

農曆三月

(April 5th - May 5th) 戊辰
Try out new things so you wouldn't be stuck with the same old routine. But as you explore new areas outside of your comfort zone, be mindful of your own limits and stay realistic.

農曆四月

(May 6th - June 5th) 己巳
You might feel like procrastinating or impulsive react without thinking but now is not the time for any of these. Focus on your goals and remain vigilant.

農曆五月

(June 6th - July 6th) 庚午
Take your time when it comes to decisions. If you don't, your impatience will only be met with more problems; therefore, think things through before anything.

農曆六月

(July 7th - August 7th) 辛未
You might find yourself travelling this month for work-related reasons. This will be a fruitful endeavour as it brings you more opportunities to increase your wealth and reputation.

農曆七月

(August 8th - September 7th) 壬申
Stressful health problems related to the stomach might appear this month so try to watch what you eat and go for medical check-ups.

農曆八月

(September 8th - October 7th) 癸酉
Be on a look out for investments that are short-termed in nature as it could prove to be financially beneficial for you.

農曆九月

(October 8th - November 7th) 甲戌
Enjoy the rise of your wealth luck this month for you would reap the rewards of your previous financial endeavours.

農曆十月

(November 8th - December 6th) 乙亥
This month, there might be an increase in competition at work. If you're in a partnership, make sure your partner is doing their share of the work by keeping an eye on them.

農曆十一月

(December 7th 2019 - January 5th 2020) 丙子
This month will prove to be difficult for married couples. Things will be tense at home as old arguments resurface.

農曆十二月

(January 6th - February 3rd 2020) 丁丑
This month, you will find new financial opportunities so make sure you work hard to give the chances that comes in your way the best shot you got.

戊子 **Wu Zi Day**

Overview

Think of this year as a fresh start for you and whatever mistakes you made in the past remains in the past. Your career outlook is looking good and there are plenty of opportunities in store for you. For business owners, it's a favourable time to go for partnerships or joint ventures. In terms of relationships, men in general are not so lucky. If you cherish your relationship, be more understanding and empathic towards your partner.

 ## Wealth

Partnerships and collaborative works are the most favourable wealth opportunities for you this year. Teamwork would be key in achieving goals that would bring about great results. Even if the reward is divided between all the parties involved, it would be more than enough for you with the added benefit of a lighter burden. Make sure you are as socially affable as possible.

 ## Relationships

If you are a single woman, you can expect to find Peach Blossom Luck in the office. However, it's only something temporary and you may still have to look for the ideal partner. Single men on the other hand would find it more favourable to look for love among his friends. For married men, they may run into some problems where third party influences would cause their wives to be suspicious of them and damage the marriage.

 ## Health

Overall, you'll be in good shape this year but your eyes and heart may cause you some minor issues. You may also gain more weight if you're not careful with managing your health. Try adopting healthy habits such as eating right and routine exercises.

 ## Career

It may not be the best year for your career, this year is at the very least an improvement compared to last year. It would be a bumpy ride getting from one end to another but this journey can be beneficial as lessons to be learned. Whatever opportunities that comes your way, make the best out of it and try to focus on the collaborative aspects of it.

農曆正月

(February 4th - March 5th) 丙寅
Women in relationships won't find this to be a good month as there might be someone who's looking to get to your partner while you're not looking.

農曆二月

(March 6th - April 4th) 丁卯
The way you interact with others need some polishing, particularly in dealing with your superior. Sometimes it's better not to say anything than to cause unnecessary trouble.

農曆三月

(April 5th - May 5th) 戊辰
Disagreements with colleagues at work are to be expected this month. Even though you don't see eye to eye on them, it is imperative to remain professional and treat each other with civility.

農曆四月

(May 6th - June 5th) 己巳
This month, you may receive a lot of opportunities to participate in social activities. But if you attend too much of them, it may drain you of your energy and affect your work.

農曆五月

(June 6th - July 6th) 庚午
It's a particularly troubling month for men in terms of their personal life as they will find women who are close to them fighting with each other. It's best to let these problems solve itself.

農曆六月

(July 7th - August 7th) 辛未
Challenges that comes your way this month should be taken with determination and grit. If you let them get the better of you, you're bound to snowball and commit worse mistakes.

農曆七月

(August 8th - September 7th) 壬申
Good wealth luck can be sustained throughout this month should you remain stable where you are and keep your eyes on your goals.

農曆八月

(September 8th - October 7th) 癸酉
Health issues would crop up this month particularly with your liver, if you're someone who consumes alcohol regularly. Some self-discipline and practicing moderation would help.

農曆九月

(October 8th - November 7th) 甲戌
This month, your partner might find themselves entangled with the law. Should you wish to help them out with it, be careful with how you involve yourself with their legal issues.

農曆十月

(November 8th - December 6th) 乙亥
Your stomach would cause you some problem this month in the form of stomach flu or food poisoning. This is particularly true if you are to travel.

農曆十一月

(December 7th 2019 - January 5th 2020) 丙子
This month, there may be a lot of people close to you who will approach you with the intention to borrow money. Don't help them beyond your capabilities.

農曆十二月

(January 6th - February 3rd 2020) 丁丑
You may be tempted this month to treat yourself a little too much which translates to going over your budget. Keep track of your spending and make sure it is within reasonable limits.

己丑 Ji Chou Day

Overview

A good year with positive results can be expected ahead. If you were born in spring, it's a particularly auspicious for you. Look for short-term investments as it would have favourable outcomes and business ventures will yield great returns. Long-term investments can be considered as well and if you're willing to be patient, the payoff will be grand.

 ## Wealth

This year, your wealth luck is shining bright, allowing you to enjoy significant gains. Just because you're in period of abundance doesn't mean you should spend your money recklessly. Have a proper plan on your budget and expenditures and look to grow your wealth with your financial windfall.

 ## Relationships

If you are a married man, your relationship is going to improve this year. For women on the other hand, trouble is brewing due to misunderstandings and arguments over communication problems.

 ## Health

You may be facing some health problems stemming from your stomach, particularly the digestive system. You may also be at risk to succumb to injuries on your head and limbs especially if you were born in summer or autumn.

Career

For all your efforts at work, you are likely to receive the well-earned recognition and acknowledgement. The people around you at your workplace will shower you with praises. Having said that, shining bright at work also means your superior would assign you with more responsibilities. Dealing with a higher set of expectation may cause your stress level to rise. It's important that you manage this aspect of your life in relation to other factors in a balance.

農曆正月

(February 4th - March 5th) 丙寅
This month, you will be rather busy with your tasks. Before you burn yourself out, take some time off every now and then to realign yourself back on track. When you have clarity of vision, you may be able to discern any plots against you from petty people at work.

農曆二月

(March 6th - April 4th) 丁卯
Those around you will be there to encourage and support you in your endeavours. Whatever you have set to achieve can be obtained easier should you reach out for help.

農曆三月

(April 5th - May 5th) 戊辰
In terms of financial luck, things are looking good this month. Consider this an opportunity to expand your wealth and formulate new ways to generate additional income. If you remain inert, these opportunities won't be able to manifest itself.

農曆四月

(May 6th - June 5th) 己巳
Whatever you have planned before in the past may crop up again. This time around, it's a much more favourable time. Try to see what you can do with them to ensure great results.

農曆五月

(June 6th - July 6th) 庚午
It will be a physically and emotionally exhaustive month for you so try to take some time off. A change of scenery would help you get back on your feet. Having said that, you should be cautious with your head as you might suffer injury on it.

農曆六月

(July 7th - August 7th) 辛未
This month you might be needing to go through a minor surgery. Scary as that may sound, it's not a big deal and your worries can be alleviated by the advice from your physician.

農曆七月

(August 8th - September 7th) 壬申
Opportunities are up for grabs only if you were to act upon them. Waiting would not be favourable for you as it requires you to be proactive in making use of these opportunities.

農曆八月

(September 8th - October 7th) 癸酉
There's a likelihood for you to receive some form of benefit or bonus at work. The catch here is that you should ask for them. This window of opportunity is not open forever so act while you can.

農曆九月

(October 8th - November 7th) 甲戌
Heated rivalry can be expected at work this month and this would cause additional stress. At the same time, you should also be mindful of your budget so that you won't be spending more than you earn.

農曆十月

(November 8th - December 6th) 乙亥
Stay true to your path and eyes on the prize. Other people might get ahead of you should you slow down so keep up the pace and continue putting in the effort.

農曆十一月

(December 7th 2019 - January 5th 2020) 丙子
There may be some changes to your immediate environment. Change can be uncomfortable but they can be beneficial as well. Have a positive outlook on your situation.

農曆十二月

(January 6th - February 3rd 2020) 丁丑
New year heralds a new start. Whatever emotional baggage you have been carrying with you, it's a good time for you to let go and start over. Create a better future for yourself free from the shackles of your past.

庚寅 **Geng Yin Day**

Geng

Yin

Overview

Increased reputation and recognition that you have long dreamed for are the perfect fruits of acknowledgement to your efforts and talents. However, one would need to have close watch on one's bank account, especially those that were born in the spring or summer, as there will be several financial issues lurking around. Do not be fret on these hurdles as you will have time and flexibility to overcome them. You may boost your wealth fortune and self-motivation by executing the travel plan or career change that you have been thinking of.

 ## Wealth

The absence of wealth fortune doesn't mean you should be discouraged from working harder, let's not forget you will still have plenty of opportunities to work hard for in life. It is okay to give up on plans that are not worthy of your effort and relocate them to better arrangements. You are advised to seek creative hobbies as they will be mostly rewarding and could even provide you with financial remuneration and mental boost as a result.

 ## Relationships

This year, single ladies should endeavour themselves to other interesting areas in life such as career and wealth as romance effort are mostly meaningless and time-wasting. Having said that, channel your energy on building better relationships with friends and family, or even to your career. Nonetheless, men who are engaged in relationships should brace themselves for potential third-party intrusion.

Health

Overall, this is generally a good year in regards of health for you! However, you should take care of your eyes, protect them and avoid spending so much time facing computer and smartphone screens. Besides, you may be more restless and depressed due to the constant stress and pressure you will be facing at work or at home in the whole year. Therefore, take better care of mental health because it is just as important as your physical health.

Career

An increase of workload is a sign that you're gaining recognition from your superior and colleagues. At the same time, you will start to feel pressure from the heavier responsibilities that you carry. Do not be shy or too harsh on yourself, ask around for advice and help if you couldn't handle things alone. It is favourable to work persistently towards your goals and career development, but you wouldn't want to pay the price of having too much stress which will damage your mental health.

農曆正月

(February 4th - March 5th) 丙寅
An excellent month is in store for you as there will be many Noble People present. Do exercise your courage to mingle around and gain genuine friendship with worthy persons.

農曆二月

(March 6th - April 4th) 丁卯
Those born during autumn and winter will experience good luck getting involved in various partnerships and other collaborative efforts.

.

農曆三月

(April 5th - May 5th) 戊辰
Your constant effort and hard work make you a standout individual, but this also cause you to become more tired over the days. As a result, things are progressing slower than they should due to your below-par energy. You are advised to participate certain activities to encourage more positive energy and to keep your spirit high.

農曆四月

(May 6th - June 5th) 己巳
You're someone who is blessed with good communication and social network skills. Therefore, channel them to the right areas such as to boost your business and wealth fortune in this month. Stay prepared and alert at all times. Remember, approach the others for their help and advices with no fear.

農曆五月

(June 6th - July 6th) 庚午
Muster the will to be more focused at work so that you do not become a victim of unscrupulous individuals who are seeking to overtake your position or spread lies about you.

農曆六月

(July 7th - August 7th) 辛未
Sudden burst of thoughts and inspirations are compass that guides you to different mentality in workplace and life. Now, splash your creative juice around as they will be rewarding.

農曆七月

(August 8th - September 7th) 壬申
Career advancement opportunity is a form of great fortune ahead at workplace, especially for individuals born during the spring or summer.

農曆八月

(September 8th - October 7th) 癸酉
Stay out of trouble and unnecessary stress by abiding the laws and ethics of the society. These practices may cost you some friends, but you wouldn't want to impress them and keep such friendships for the price of legal punishment either. Unscrupulous individuals are not worthy of your time and effort.

農曆九月

(October 8th - November 7th) 甲戌
You have done so much work thus far, so don't be too harsh on yourself. Give yourself a break this month and enjoy life as it is.

農曆十月

(November 8th - December 6th) 乙亥
Think before you act is always the best advice when it comes to making a decision on complex matters. Therefore, do not discuss the problems in advance and never be stubborn for inappropriate beliefs.

農曆十一月

(December 7th 2019 - January 5th 2020) 丙子
Healthy teamwork will prove to be beneficial for you. Your relationships with your peers will be strengthened and everyone will learn valuable interpersonal skills.

農曆十二月

(January 6th - February 3rd 2020) 丁丑
You will come across more leisure and spare time which might be partly temptations. Do not waste these valuable times for non-beneficial activities. Instead, set some restrictions in life and refrain yourself from activities with negative effects.

六十甲子 Forecast for 2019 based on Day of Birth

辛卯 Xin Mao Day

Overview

This year, you might find unexpected opportunities in your career. In order to make the best out of them, you have to be ready for anything and make plans for everything. Your talents can be improved by taking on new skills and experimenting with new ideas. If you own a business, it's time for you to change your ways in order to improve your results.

 ## Wealth

It would be favourable for you this year to invest in some assets so have that in your consideration. At the same time, manage a budget to make sure your finances are on track. Try your best to avoid impulsive spending. Invest in things that you know with certainty that it will be profitable.

 ## Relationships

When it comes to romance, men will have more Peach Blossom Luck than women. Women in particular need to prepare for turmoil in their relationship. Take this time for some introspection and ask yourself if all the arguments are truly necessary.

 ## Health

Your health is looking overall this year but it doesn't mean you shouldn't keep your guard up. You're still susceptible to food or skin related allergies. Minor as they may be, there's no harm in minding what you eat. Try to go for a healthier lifestyle such as adopting better diet and exercise habits.

 ## Career

If you feel like you need a career change, this year would be good to do as you've accumulated much recognition for your skills and talent. Your ideas can go far and wide should you choose to market them properly. With that in mind, it would be ideal for you to improve your communication and presentation skills. However, you seem to have a temper when your boss is in the picture. Remain professional and practice diplomacy.

農曆正月

(February 4th - March 5th) 丙寅
Wealth isn't looking so great for you this month. Consider finding out new ways to create additional income.

農曆二月

(March 6th - April 4th) 丁卯
Who you consider to be your worst rivals could be your greatest allies. Try to collaborate something with them and see what happens.

農曆三月

(April 5th - May 5th) 戊辰
You might feel like procrastinating, but it won't do you any good. If anything, it will only set you back with work that should've been done.

農曆四月

(May 6th - June 5th) 己巳
Your patience is limited this month so try not to put yourself in situations where it would be tested to avoid outburst. At the same time, you will have wealth luck this month.

農曆五月

(June 6th - July 6th) 庚午
Should you focus too much in your pursuing wealth, it will take a toll on your personal relationship. Always remember to set some time for that so it won't be neglected.

農曆六月

(July 7th - August 7th) 辛未
For men who have been in long-term relationships for a while, it's a good month for you to finally make it official.

農曆七月

(August 8th - September 7th) 壬申
Encouragement and support from your boss would be vital for you in terms of future financial endeavours.

農曆八月

(September 8th - October 7th) 癸酉
You can expect a potential career advancement or a pay raise at work this month.

農曆九月

(October 8th - November 7th) 甲戌
If you feel like experimenting or trying out new things, it's a good month for you to do so. Go out and discover new things.

農曆十月

(November 8th - December 6th) 乙亥
Chances are, this month you will be travelling. At the same time, you might encounter minor health issues such as stomach flu or allergies.

農曆十一月

(December 7th 2019 - January 5th 2020) 丙子
Safeguard yourself from any impulse spending. It might feel good temporarily but you will come to regret its lasting repercussion.

農曆十二月

(January 6th - February 3rd 2020) 丁丑
Keep an open mind this month as you might be inspired by your colleagues at work that may have good ideas that are beneficial for you.

壬辰 **Ren Chen Day**

Overview

This year would rather uneventful for you. If you were born in autumn, you may be affected by legal issues so try to be more cautious in order to avoid unwanted problems. When it comes to working with others, don't be afraid to participate as social endeavours are favourable to you. Set aside some money in case you have to use it for possible health problems.

 ## Wealth

Generally, your wealth luck is alright. However, the details might catch you off-guard if you're not careful, leading you to unfavourable outcomes. As such, in any activity that you get yourself involved in, take everything into account and avoid shortcuts. Work hard in maintaining whatever good you have right now.

 ## Relationships

In terms of romance, those who are single may find someone special this year. But if you are married, there's a possibility for third party temptations. Stay true to your vows as it would not be worth it for you to destroy your current relationship over short-term enjoyment.

 ## Health

You may be going through surgery in this year. Fret not, as it would be minor in nature and you would be able to be back on your feet after a short rest. Try to make sure that your health is one of the top priority as you may face certain problems such as stomach issues. Be thankful for your good health and remember to take preventative measures before the problems appear.

 ## Career

Your career would have a considerable improvement and this is particularly true for those born in spring. For everyone else, they can expect increase in workload which may lead to unhappiness and anxiety. From time to time, give yourself a break and catch your breath.

農曆正月

(February 4th - March 5th) 丙寅
Your ideas and position might be challenged by others this month. When that happens, prepare to defend yourself and continue with what you have planned.

農曆二月

(March 6th - April 4th) 丁卯
Expect fever or sore throat this month especially for those born during the summer season.

農曆三月

(April 5th - May 5th) 戊辰
You may expect great rewards from financial opportunities this month. Bear in mind that this is achievable only through the help of others and teamwork.

農曆四月

(May 6th - June 5th) 己巳
Positive career luck awaits those born during spring. You may be able to receive a promotion or at least a pay raise.

農曆五月

(June 6th - July 6th) 庚午
You may be facing a considerable amount of stress during work this month because of an increase in the amount of responsibilities. Make sure your time is managed properly to avoid overworking yourself.

農曆六月

(July 7th - August 7th) 辛未
You may be going through surgery this month. Try not to panic and discuss the options and procedure carefully with your physician so that it would take some of the fear away.

農曆七月

(August 8th - September 7th) 壬申
At work, you might be finding yourself going through some battles all on your own. Don't be lazy or procrastinate as it won't help you in your cause.

農曆八月

(September 8th - October 7th) 癸酉
When handling tools or activities that are potentially harmful, practice caution as there's a chance for you to injure yourself.

農曆九月

(October 8th - November 7th) 甲戌
Learn how to spread out your responsibilities to other capable and willing people. In doing so, there will be less stress on your part and more productivity overall.

農曆十月

(November 8th - December 6th) 乙亥
Now's a good time to go for a holiday and take some time off. Consider it as a reward for your efforts and hard work.

農曆十一月

(December 7th 2019 - January 5th 2020) 丙子
This month, your ideas would provide you with favourable financial outcomes. Don't hesitate to initiate and realise what you have in mind.

農曆十二月

(January 6th - February 3rd 2020) 丁丑
Keep your budget tight this month and spend only when you need to. Save up your money as spontaneous spending would have negative effects on your wealth for a long time.

癸巳 Gui Si Day

Overview

Think of this year as a fresh start for you and whatever mistakes you made in the past remains in the past. Your career outlook is looking good and there are plenty of opportunities in store for you. For business owners, it's a favourable time to go for partnerships or joint ventures. In terms of relationships, men in general are not so lucky. If you cherish your relationship, be more understanding and empathic towards your partner.

 ## Wealth

Partnerships and collaborative works are the most favourable wealth opportunities for you this year. Teamwork would be key in achieving goals that would bring about great results. Even if the reward is divided between all the parties involved, it would be more than enough for you with the added benefit of a lighter burden. Make sure you are as socially affable as possible.

 ## Relationships

If you are a single woman, you can expect to find Peach Blossom Luck in the office. However, it's only something temporary and you may still have to look for the ideal partner. Single men on the other hand would find it more favourable to look for love among his friends. For married men, they may run into some problems where third party influences would cause their wives to be suspicious of them and damage the marriage.

 ## Health

Overall, you'll be in good shape this year but your eyes and heart may cause you some minor issues. You may also gain more weight if you're not careful with managing your health. Try adopting healthy habits such as eating right and routine exercises.

 ## Career

It may not be the best year for your career, this year is at the very least an improvement compared to last year. It would be a bumpy ride getting from one end to another but this journey can be beneficial as lessons to be learned. Whatever opportunities that comes your way, make the best out of it and try to focus on the collaborative aspects of it.

農曆正月

(February 4th - March 5th) 丙寅
Women in relationships won't find this to be a good month as there might be someone who's looking to get to your partner while you're not looking.

農曆二月

(March 6th - April 4th) 丁卯
The way you interact with others need some polishing, particularly in dealing with your superior. Sometimes it's better not to say anything than to cause unnecessary trouble.

農曆三月

(April 5th - May 5th) 戊辰
Disagreements with colleagues at work are to be expected this month. Even though you don't see eye to eye on them, it is imperative to remain professional and treat each other with civility.

農曆四月

(May 6th - June 5th) 己巳
This month, you may receive a lot of opportunities to participate in social activities. But if you attend too much of them, it may drain you of your energy and affect your work.

農曆五月

(June 6th - July 6th) 庚午
It's a particularly troubling month for men in terms of their personal life as they will find women who are close to them fighting with each other. It's best to let these problems solve itself.

農曆六月

(July 7th - August 7th) 辛未
Challenges that comes your way this month should be taken with determination and grit. If you let them get the better of you, you're bound to snowball and commit worse mistakes.

農曆七月

(August 8th - September 7th) 壬申
Good wealth luck can be sustained throughout this month should you remain stable where you are and keep your eyes on your goals.

農曆八月

(September 8th - October 7th) 癸酉
Health issues would crop up this month particularly with your liver, if you're someone who consumes alcohol regularly. Some self-discipline and practicing moderation would help.

農曆九月

(October 8th - November 7th) 甲戌
This month, your partner might find themselves entangled with the law. Should you wish to help them out with it, be careful with how you involve yourself with their legal issues.

農曆十月

(November 8th - December 6th) 乙亥
Your stomach would cause you some problem this month in the form of stomach flu or food poisoning. This is particularly true if you are to travel.

農曆十一月

(December 7th 2019 - January 5th 2020) 丙子
This month, there may be a lot of people close to you who will approach you with the intention to borrow money. Don't help them beyond your capabilities.

農曆十二月

(January 6th - February 3rd 2020) 丁丑
You may be tempted this month to treat yourself a little too much which translates to going over your budget. Keep track of your spending and make sure it is within reasonable limits.

甲午 Jia Wu Day

Overview

Winter season babies may find this a rocky year since there are plenty of hurdles ahead. You might be demotivated or deflated while working towards your goals. Nonetheless, don't be too harsh on yourself and relax over the less satisfied results. Instead, channel your focus to work as there are various opportunities up for grab this year.

 ## Wealth

Your wealth fortune seems rather less impressive this year. As such, investments would prove to be unwise at this time. If you need to put your money somewhere, property would be a safe choice to go for. Do not play any financial guessing game as it will only fruit negative result. Think before you act will allow you to survive the year for good.

 ## Relationships

Single male individuals have better chance to embrace their romance lives this year. Connections from mom may bring good choice for you. That being said, female individuals, will encounter speed bump while looking for love. This is because one may be over self-protective and cautious which discourage the approach of others. You are allow to be vulnerable at times, and others will explore your true personalities from there.

 ## Health

Heart and blood pressures problems are your two primary health concerns if you are forty and above. Others will experience a rather moderate health condition. That being said, never take things for granted and schedule yourself for frequent medical check-ups to tackle the early illness signs or symptoms. Also, chances are some will encounter eye issues too.

 ## Career

Be firm and confident in making decisions especially the career ones. Never pack too much of targets together as this will cause you to lose focus and harder to achieve the goals. Besides, unwise plans and decision also leave you unnecessary issues to deal with. Arrange your career path wisely to focus more on the tasks given rather than the rewards.

農曆正月

(February 4th - March 5th) 丙寅
Things may seem tempting as first, but some opportunities definitely don't worth your time and effort. Consider your options cautiously and be thoughtful of making the appropriate decision.

農曆二月

(March 6th - April 4th) 丁卯
Individuals who particularly born during winter season will stumble across law issues that will give you tough time. Never ignore these problems and look for solutions immediately before things lose their control.

農曆三月

(April 5th - May 5th) 戊辰
It's okay to prioritise yourself at times. Spend this month to enhance your confidence and accept compliments with courtesy. Remember, it is never a bad thing to have a strong sense of self-belief.

農曆四月

(May 6th - June 5th) 己巳
Individuals that are married are prone to gossips and rumours about their relationship this month. That being said, do not let these problems to affect you and focus only on your own work and business.

農曆五月

(June 6th - July 6th) 庚午
The presence of Noble People is an auspicious sign as they will assist you to achieve your goals or to keep you away from trouble. Never afraid to ask for help when you cannot deal things alone as the Noble People have more experience to help you out.

農曆六月

(July 7th - August 7th) 辛未
This is a month to work for the teamwork between you and your peers. Excellent collaboration helps ease your burden and contribute efficient method for tasks to make them more exciting and promising.

農曆七月

(August 8th - September 7th) 壬申
Tensions are building in professional relationships this month. Workplace atmosphere can be awkward, thus individuals should be honest and diplomatic at this time. Things will get along with better communication and effective discussion.

農曆八月

(September 8th - October 7th) 癸酉
Chances are you are looking for new social circles to mingle around, signifying social developments in this month. Nevertheless, never ignore your responsibilities or overindulge in parties to avoid an imbalanced life.

農曆九月

(October 8th - November 7th) 甲戌
Hesitation and over-suspicion on hard decision may cause important windows to close on you. That being said, be open-minded with your choice and embrace the upcoming opportunities with preparation. Make wise decisions while proceeding.

農曆十月

(November 8th - December 6th) 乙亥
Decisions regarding finance should be avoided this month as you are not in the right mentality to make such crucial changes at this stage. Be patient and wait for the appropriate time to raise the issues and act accordingly.

農曆十一月

(December 7th 2019 - January 5th 2020) 丙子
Auspicious turn of fortune are in sight in the form of year end promotion for you. Speaking of which, you shall focus on keeping the momentum going and stay thoughtful on your appearance and impression to the others at work.

農曆十二月

(January 6th - February 3rd 2020) 丁丑
Chances are you will be faced with possible road accidents or other legal issues. As prevention is better than a cure, you should obey the traffic rules strictly and focus on road safety at all costs.

乙未 Yi Wei Day

Yi

Wei

Overview
This year would be relatively comfortable for you with not too many drastic bumps that would put you in difficult positions. At the same time, changes that are positive would also take time to happen. Any promotion or acknowledge at work would come slow. You should take this as an opportunity for you to solidify your base and plan for the future.

 ### Wealth
In terms of wealth, it's somewhat stagnant this year. Just because it's not going anywhere doesn't mean you should give up. On the contrary, you should keep up the pace you're going as your efforts will be rewarded sooner or later.

 ### Relationships
When it comes to love, it's not going anywhere either. But, this also means you have more time to spend on enhancing other aspects of your life. If you are already in a relationship and you're not entirely happy, try to appreciate each other for what they bring into the relationship by spending more time together.

 ### Health
In general, this year you will have good health. However, you are still susceptible to minor eye-related issues. As soon as any symptom appear, seek medical attention. You may also encounter injury to your limbs if you're not too careful with activities that involve them.

 ### Career
If you are planning to change jobs this year, put it on hold and stay where you are. It is unfavourable for you to change now and it is much more rewarding if you continue being industrious. Your efforts will be rewarded later on.

農曆正月

(February 4th - March 5th) 丙寅
This year, your financial luck shines bright, particularly for those born during winter. Should you find yourself travelling this month, make sure you don't overspend by keeping your eye on your expenditures.

農曆二月

(March 6th - April 4th) 丁卯
Wealth luck continues to be improving this month. At the same time, you shouldn't take this opportunity for granted. Instead, be more assertive in achieving your goals and keep up with the pace.

農曆三月

(April 5th - May 5th) 戊辰
When you have already achieving what you set out to do, maintain your hard work. Just because you are already rewarded doesn't mean you should slow down. Make sure your senses remain sharp so that you may achieve more goals in the future.

農曆四月

(May 6th - June 5th) 己巳
Your well-earned success may attract unsavoury rumours from those who are petty. Don't bother with these sorts of people and focus on continuing your good work.

農曆五月

(June 6th - July 6th) 庚午
Rivalries will escalate at workplace, hindering both your work and progress. Stay determined and you will be able to get through these troubling times.

農曆六月

(July 7th - August 7th) 辛未
You may feel like doubting yourself this month. Believe in your own abilities and give yourself more credit based on your prior achievements. This will build up your confidence and deter hesitation.

農曆七月

(August 8th - September 7th) 壬申
Your life at the moment may see confusing with everything that's going on at the same time. This may affect your decision-making abilities and prolonging problems.

農曆八月

(September 8th - October 7th) 癸酉
This month, you will be afflicted by bouts of mood swings which may manifest itself as volatile emotions. Keep your temper under control in confrontations in order not to aggravate the matter.

農曆九月

(October 8th - November 7th) 甲戌
For men who are in relationships, you may be tempted to stray from your fidelity to your significant other this month. Think through your situation with clear thought, then make the right decision to stay loyal and cherish what you have.

農曆十月

(November 8th - December 6th) 乙亥
It's a good time for you to be travelling this month. One possible reason to do so would be work-related. It may potentially be financially rewarding and at the same time a change of scenery is nice.

農曆十一月

(December 7th 2019 - January 5th 2020) 丙子
Before you decide on any paperwork or official documents, pay attention to every single detail cautiously to avoid trouble with the law. You may also want to detach yourself from the negative influence of certain people around you.

農曆十二月

(January 6th - February 3rd 2020) 丁丑
When you're trying to get your work done, your boss might be in your way. This would cause you some discomfort. You may try to resolve the matter with proper communication with your superior and reach a mutual understanding.

丙申 **Bing Shen Day**

Overview

You can expect much progress and rewards from all your hard work this year including chances to travel for your career. Make the most out of this by extending your circle of networks to open doors for future opportunities. Bear in mind that you shouldn't let your ego get the best of you. For students, academic success is in the bag provided they put in the effort.

 ## Wealth

You may overspend if you're not careful with your budget so practice restrain this year. You might feel like spending some money to make yourself happy, but it would be temporary as you would have to deal with the repercussion eventually. If you consider investments this year, keep it short-term and risk free.

 ## Relationships

This year, your relationship wouldn't be smooth sailing. As much as those around you are inclined to help you out with your problems, they will only aggravate the matter. In terms of relationship luck, women will have it better than men. Those who are married should put their trust and faith in each other and not rely on hearsay.

 ## Health

Relatively speaking, your health is somewhat stable this year. You might experience some hearing or vision problems, but they're nothing damning. If you are in your mid-thirties or older, you might have some issues with your blood pressure. Try to take up exercising, better diet and overall a healthier lifestyle.

 ## Career

For those in education, career progression is around the corner this year. Establish strong relationships with your peers and superior to ensure future success by planning strategically. Be careful with your words as it might unknowingly offend someone. Keep your emotions and actions in check as to maintain a professional, yet warm relationship with your colleagues.

農曆正月

(February 4th - March 5th) 丙寅
You may consider looking for new ways to generate wealth this month holds strong financial prospects for you.

農曆二月

(March 6th - April 4th) 丁卯
If you were born in summer, your health might take a hit by some minor diseases such as sore throat or fever.

農曆三月

(April 5th - May 5th) 戊辰
For those born in winter, expect career progression this month in the form of promotion or bonuses as you may have positive luck in career prospects.

農曆四月

(May 6th - June 5th) 己巳
This month might be difficult to handle as workload might overwhelm you but try not to burn out. Tackle the job one at a time to make progress and at the same time take breaks for yourself every now and then.

農曆五月

(June 6th - July 6th) 庚午
You can expect a boost in creativity this month as you may be able to come up with new ideas easily. You might want to consider taking advantage of this by coming up with new ways to generate income.

農曆六月

(July 7th - August 7th) 辛未
Your workload will increase this month, leading to stress. Your colleagues might be able to help lighten your burden if you seek help from them.

農曆七月

(August 8th - September 7th) 壬申
Careful with your words and action this month as there may be people who are looking to take credit for your work and steal your ideas.

農曆八月

(September 8th - October 7th) 癸酉
There is a risk of health problems for pregnant women this month, so exercise some caution. For everyone else in general, the right side of the body is vulnerable.

農曆九月

(October 8th - November 7th) 甲戌
Your life may change in some way as you're finally determined enough to break out of certain habits. Try out new things as changes are likely to have positive results.

農曆十月

(November 8th - December 6th) 乙亥
Take a more passive stance this month with your actions. Be strategic and cover all your bases. This month, risks are not worth it as you might deal with issues you didn't account for.

農曆十一月

(December 7th 2019 - January 5th 2020) 丙子
Your relationship might suffer from you spending more time on your career. Make sure your loved ones are not ignored, try to manage your time in a way that you can balance both your personal and professional life.

農曆十二月

(January 6th - February 3rd 2020) 丁丑
Your stomach is susceptible to illness such as digestive issues or stomach flue this month. You can avoid these problems if you were to be careful with the food you eat.

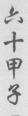

丁酉 **Ding You Day**

Ding

You

Overview

You will find this year to be especially tiring and busy. This would likely lead to stress and at the same time, some of it would come from your family as well. Therefore, it is important at times to step back, unwind and relax to get yourself back on your feet. Once you make it through the tough times, you will make easy progress.

Wealth

As your wealth luck is unfavourable for this year, be mindful of your financial spending. Make sure to keep track of your budget and plan ahead in order to avoid over-spending. If you are born in the summer, however, this effect is less pronounced.

Relationships

If you're considering to settle down and start a family, this would be an ideal year for you. But should you decide to do so, you must be clear of mind and ready to compromise. Take into consideration the concerns and needs of others. Married women in particular need to watch out for potential problems.

Health

This would be a good time for you to take note of what food you're consuming and stop eating unhealthily, especially if you were born in winter. After ridding yourself of junk food, perhaps you could go on detox in order to cleanse your system; allowing yourself to have a fresh start. This will definitely help in curbing your bad habits in the long run.

Career

If you focus on your career goals this year, your effort will be rewarded. As long as you can ignore distractions, productivity and progress will be gained quickly. You might even get a job promotion if you remain committed to your goals.

農曆正月

(February 4th - March 5th) 丙寅
For this month, your financial outlook is positive. It's a chance for you to take one or two additional sources of income.

農曆二月

(March 6th - April 4th) 丁卯
You will find that your previous month luck would continue. As such, it would be wise to make full use of any opportunities that you receive.

農曆三月

(April 5th - May 5th) 戊辰
Communication will be a difficulty for you in this month. This will lead to unstable relationships, especially with your superiors at work. Try your best to make sure whatever it is you're trying to say is understood to prevent misunderstanding.

農曆四月

(May 6th - June 5th) 己巳
Keep an eye out for any legal issue that might appear this month. If you don't settle them immediately, it might grow worse and cause you worse problems in the future.

農曆五月

(June 6th - July 6th) 庚午
Be open to the advice and opinion from those around you. You will find support and people who are receptive of your ideas and they will gladly offer you assistance with them.

農曆六月

(July 7th - August 7th) 辛未
As you are more susceptible to food poisoning this month, lookout on what and where you eat. Make sure the food that you eat is hygienic.

農曆七月

(August 8th - September 7th) 壬申
In this month, it is likely your spouse may do something that would upset you. You should however keep your emotions in check in order to keep the problems at a minimum.

農曆八月

(September 8th - October 7th) 癸酉
Pay attention to the details of legal documents this month, especially ones that require a signature. Read exactly what it says before you commit as you might find yourself in trouble over a tiny detail that you could miss out.

農曆九月

(October 8th - November 7th) 甲戌
You will find yourself calmer as this is a month of clarity and balance. As self-awareness will come to you naturally, it's a good time to re-examine yourself to find your own faults and flaws in order to make some self-improvement.

農曆十月

(November 8th - December 6th) 乙亥
As it is not a good month to be spontaneous, don't give into your impulses. Before you say or do anything, think carefully as every action has consequences.

農曆十一月

(December 7th 2019 - January 5th 2020) 丙子
You may be tempted to make some quick cash by ignoring the rules, but it's not worth it. The consequences will be heavy if you do not refrain yourself from taking the improper way to wealth.

農曆十二月

(January 6th - February 3rd 2020) 丁丑
For married men, they will be tied down at work with a busy schedule that takes them away from their family, making it a difficult month for them. The needs of their families would only add on more pressure to them.

六十甲子

Forecast for 2019 based on Day of Birth

戊戌 Wu Xu Day

Overview

It's an important year for you to grow in terms of your career and getting to where you want to be. In your journey, you might be met with unwanted problems such as rumours or gossip by those who want to see you fail. Be mentally prepared for such tribulations and learn to focus on your goals rather than getting tangled in these petty things. Have a group of people whom you can rely on to make sure your success is secured.

Wealth

For those born during spring or summer, anything that involves working with other people would be fruitful for you. Make use of these collaborative endeavours to solidify your relationships and form a strong social network. Take the time to come up with new and exciting ways to turn an unfavourable situation into a favourable one and make substantial progress.

Relationships

In terms of relationship, you might be run into some problems in the form of competition. Focus on increasing your own value in order to deter any third-party influence. If you're already in a relationship, stay loyal to each other and work on the relationship together.

Health

Overall, your health would be good this year but do keep your blood pressure and diet in check. Besides your physical aspect, pay attention to your mental wellbeing as well because it might manifest itself as an illness. Be wary of skin allergies and eye-related problems.

Career

Teamwork and collaborative endeavours will help you in your career. In doing so, make sure it is not compromised by your emotions and it may affect a potential promotion in the works negatively. For entrepreneurs, this year might be difficult. Stay focused to your goals and you will be able to make it through this year just fine.

農曆正月

(February 4th - March 5th) 丙寅
Keep your eyes out as you might miss out on opportunities that comes your way. Be more aware of your surroundings.

農曆二月

(March 6th - April 4th) 丁卯
Share your ideas freely with others or else your work might not be going anywhere. This is not the time for you to keep them to yourself so don't worry about it.

農曆三月

(April 5th - May 5th) 戊辰
In order for you to receive a possible promotion this month, you need to put your back in It and persevere. Stay determined and you will reap your reward.

農曆四月

(May 6th - June 5th) 己巳
When it comes to romance this months, things might get complicated. Even so, don't let it affect other aspects of your life especially the one at work.

農曆五月

(June 6th - July 6th) 庚午
Someone close to you might want to borrow money this month. Be more careful with your finances especially if you are in a partnership.

農曆六月

(July 7th - August 7th) 辛未
This month, you might find a surprising insight or information from a friend. Keep in mind not to take advantage or exploit them for their ideas.

農曆七月

(August 8th - September 7th) 壬申
This might be a troubling month for you in terms of your emotions. Stay cool and not let your temper get the better of you and make sure your decisions are unaffected by your mood swings.

農曆八月

(September 8th - October 7th) 癸酉
There is a chance of food poisoning should you travel north this month so try to be careful with what you eat.

農曆九月

(October 8th - November 7th) 甲戌
It will be beneficial for you this month should you try out new activities. Do not hesitate to take the first step and take innovative approaches.

農曆十月

(November 8th - December 6th) 乙亥
Don't let your pride get the best of you as you may put yourself in unfavourable position. Stay clear from making any decision until your emotions are stabilised.

農曆十一月
(December 7th 2019 - January 5th 2020) 丙子
Teamwork and collaboration would do you good as you would be sharing your workload with others, making it easier overall for greater rewards. This is particularly true if you were born in summer.

農曆十二月

(January 6th - February 3rd 2020) 丁丑
You shouldn't let your career life affect your relationships negatively. Always remember those you care about and don't let them be neglected.

己亥 **Ji Hai Day**

己
Ji
亥
Hai

Overview
Much progress can be made in your life as you will find many opportunities that are yours for the taking this year. However, be warned that your past may come back to haunt you in the form of legal troubles. Aside from that, you will also experience stress from the process of trying to achieve your goals. All these factors can be harmful to your health. It would be imperative for you to juggle your responsibilities with balance.

 ## Wealth
There is a strong possibility this year that you will gain financial wealth. At the same time, don't put all your eggs in one basket as there may be hidden opportunities coming your way. In the process of making money, don't take any shortcuts or obtain it illicitly. Breaking the law is never worth it. Play it safe and keep yourself clean.

 ## Relationships
An emotionally turbulent year awaits you if you are a man. After the rain comes sunshine however as the relationship will be strengthened should you brave the storm. As for women in general, they would need to learn balancing their relationship with other aspects of their life. It's important that you do not let one aspect influence another negatively.

Health
Your liver would be your main concern this year in regards to your health. Practice moderation when it comes to alcohol and take good care of your health. Be on a lookout for tumours and growths as well.

Career
If you were born in spring, then you may expect this year to be good for your career. You need to remember that you don't have to take everything on by yourself. Allow others to help you out so that your burden would be reduced. The people around you are more than willy to lend a hand.

農曆正月

(February 4th - March 5th) 丙寅
If you need any help this month, look to your colleagues as they will prove to be resourceful and comforting. Take what they say to heart and collaborate together to make their ideas happen.

農曆二月

(March 6th - April 4th) 丁卯
There's a possibility this month for women to experience gynaecological issues. Preventative measures should be taken before it gets serious by going to regular medical check-ups.

農曆三月

(April 5th - May 5th) 戊辰
This month, you might find yourself bored with both work and relationship as they stagnate. Rather than waiting for the situation to improve on its own, take the more active approach and initiate the change for the better yourself.

農曆四月

(May 6th - June 5th) 己巳
In the process of trying to get what you want, you may be tempted to throw your ethics out the window. Remember to always do the right thing before you consider making regrettable decisions.

農曆五月

(June 6th - July 6th) 庚午
If you were born in spring, your career might advance this month. For everyone else born in summer, autumn and winter however, you get to experience stress instead.

農曆六月

(July 7th - August 7th) 辛未
This month, you need to pay attention to your health issues. Make sure everything is in top shape. There's also a possibility that you might need to pay the dentist a visit.

農曆七月

(August 8th - September 7th) 壬申
This would be a good month for you to pick up a new skill and diversify your talents. Find the resources necessary for you to gain new information such as events, talks, short classes and your life would be more colourful afterwards.

農曆八月

(September 8th - October 7th) 癸酉
Before you do or decide on anything this month, think it through carefully. Acting impulsively right now will only produce negative outcomes.

農曆九月

(October 8th - November 7th) 甲戌
You might find that some people are simply too good to be true. It would be right for you to doubt them as they may be insincere with ulterior motives to take advantage of you.

農曆十月

(November 8th - December 6th) 乙亥
Now would be a good time for you to travel and it would be favourable for you to head south. Try to make this happen as the experience would be beneficial for you.

農曆十一月

(December 7th 2019 - January 5th 2020) 丙子
Your relationship would be rather unstable this month as things get tense. The cause of the problem lies in trust issues and jealousy. Approach this problem carefully with empathy and honesty.

農曆十二月

(January 6th - February 3rd 2020) 丁丑
Everyone deserves a break every now and then and right now it would be ideal for you to do so. Relax and enjoy yourself, take the time to catch your breath and get yourself back on track.

庚子 Geng Zi Day

Overview

You might have to adapt to changes in your life that will make this year rather difficult for you. How you handle these changes and where you stand in the face of uncertainty will require you to be more assertive. It would be favourable for you if you go for opportunities that is related to your wealth. While you would be exhausted from spending your resources this year, it will pay off for you eventually.

 ## Wealth

Money won't come easy for you this year and a lot of effort is required. Rather than waiting for opportunities to come to you, you may be able to make it for yourself by innovating your style of work or old projects. You may turn to those around you to find inspiration on how to execute your creativity. Your financial position would benefit should you practice teamwork with other people.

 ## Relationships

Peach Blossom Luck would be better for men this year but if they wish to see results, they need to be proactive about it. One way to help you in your search for romance would be through the help of friends or acquaintances. Single women on the other hand should rely more on themselves than others in finding their ideal partner. They are more likely to find love should they travel.

 ## Health

Your health requires your attention this year, particularly the second half of the year. By then, you would find yourself weaker than usual. Your immune system may require some strengthening, perhaps through regular exercise and healthier diet. Watch out for your legs as they are susceptible to injuries and as such be careful with activities that requires them.

 ## Career

Let your creativity loose with work this year and you may find yourself ahead of the competition. Have back up plans ready so that you would be adapt to any circumstances that you find yourself in or any sudden changes in your work environment. There's a strong likelihood of change to happen to you in terms of work this year.

農曆正月

(February 4th - March 5th) 丙寅
Expect rivalry to ramp up at work this month. As such, do your best in getting the job done so that others won't overtake you.

農曆二月

(March 6th - April 4th) 丁卯
As your career luck is not looking good this month, you would have negative outcome if you to close any business deals or attend important meetings.

農曆三月

(April 5th - May 5th) 戊辰
Plan and strategize well this month with innovative new ideas that would be practical in any situation so that you may adapt to anything that comes your way.

農曆四月

(May 6th - June 5th) 己巳
Now would be a good time for you to travel. Travelling would inspire you with new ideas and fresh new perspectives. At the same time, you might fall in while travelling at the same time so be careful with your health.

農曆五月

(June 6th - July 6th) 庚午
This month, you will have a favourable outcome should you try to earn some additional income. If you were born in spring or summer, expect bouts of mood swings.

農曆六月

(July 7th - August 7th) 辛未
A challenging month awaits men as their relationships will be strained. Disagreements and quarrelling gets more common and stress naturally follows. Make sure your emotions doesn't compel you to do or say anything regrettable.

農曆七月

(August 8th - September 7th) 壬申
If you were born in autumn or winter, there's a possibility this month that you would be susceptible to health issues. On the plus side, your wealth luck would be strong at the same time.

農曆八月

(September 8th - October 7th) 癸酉
It would be beneficial for your health and wealth should you travel southwards this month. A get away will allow you to recuperate and at the same time fill you with new ideas.

農曆九月

(October 8th - November 7th) 甲戌
This month, your creativity will flow as you are enlightened with new ideas that you may present to your colleagues at your workplace.

農曆十月

(November 8th - December 6th) 乙亥
Take some time off this month to rest and get yourself back on your feet. Your mental and physical health are important and you should take good care of them.

農曆十一月

(December 7th 2019 - January 5th 2020) 丙子
You might need to put in some extra effort at work this month as competition heats up. Don't resort to unethical shortcuts to complete your goals. If you try to bring yourself up by taking others down, sooner or later you will live to pay for the consequences.

農曆十二月

(January 6th - February 3rd 2020) 丁丑
There's a chance that others may speak badly about you behind your back this month. Change your perspective to see that they're doing this because you are doing better than them and as such the negativity should be ignored.

 **Xin Chou Day**

Overview

This year, you can expect both the good and bad coming from career advancement. With new responsibilities comes new challenges to face. You will have to persevere in the face of these difficulties and take the initiative in finding ways to handle them. These problems will require you in a leadership role in order to get them solved.

 ### Wealth

In terms of wealth, there will be many obstacles in your way. Despite other people not honouring their end of the deal, do not be disheartened. Instead, remain focused on your goals and move on when these things happen. Instead of holding on to past transgressions, look forward and find ways to make sure your future endeavours are better.

 ### Relationships

Your relationship might suffer this year unless you pay more attention to it. No relationships are perfect and any problems that can be overcome together is a chance for the relationship to grow stronger. For men, they should try not to put their career before their relationship too frequently.

Health

Health concerns shouldn't be much of an issue overall. There are still chances for minor annoyances with your kidneys or recurring skin irritations. One possible suspect would be due to an allergy, so try to identify the problem early on in order to avoid it.

Career

A career change is suitable to occur this year if it's something you've been considering. Take the initiative and strategize properly when it comes to looking for new prospects. A new work environment would reignite your sense of passion and purpose. Keep the momentum going after the change to ensure continuous quality work from yourself.

農曆正月

(February 4th - March 5th) 丙寅
If you were born in summer, be on a lookout for those seeking to backstab by spoiling your plans you this month.

農曆二月

(March 6th - April 4th) 丁卯
This month, you might be faced with temptations to burst out in anger. Try the best you can to keep your head cool as there are repercussions for letting your emotions take control.

農曆三月

(April 5th - May 5th) 戊辰
For those who are married, some changes in their lives this month will cause tension. Deal with this according and make proper adjustments.

農曆四月

(May 6th - June 5th) 己巳
Positive wealth luck can be expected this month. Even so, if you would like to reap its benefits you still have to work for it.

農曆五月

(June 6th - July 6th) 庚午
If you were born in autumn or winter, the positive wealth luck continues this month. Take the opportunity to seize any available financial prospect.

農曆六月

(July 7th - August 7th) 辛未
If you feel like a project you're working on is finished, take some time to make sure there aren't any loose ends. You might suffer if there are things you overlooked. Keep your emotions under control and decide everything carefully with a clear mind.

農曆七月

(August 8th - September 7th) 壬申
Your relationship might be threatened by a third party this month. Practice honesty with your partner and be clear with how you truly feel to avoid misunderstanding.

農曆八月

(September 8th - October 7th) 癸酉
This month, you will struggle with coughs, weak lungs and other respiratory issues. For single men who are looking for a partner, potential complications await them.

農曆九月

(October 8th - November 7th) 甲戌
You might be overwhelmed by the amount of workload this month. Remember to set aside some time for yourself every now and then.

農曆十月

(November 8th - December 6th) 乙亥
Whatever plans you have made might go through some changes this month. It's best that you prepare additional backup plans so you can be ready for anything.

農曆十一月

(December 7th 2019 - January 5th 2020) 丙子
Be careful with who you share your ideas to as there may be people this month who are not above claiming your work as their own.

農曆十二月

(January 6th - February 3rd 2020) 丁丑
Instead of talking behind your colleagues or reacting to them with hostility, be direct and communicate with honesty and professionalism.

壬寅 Ren Yin Day

Overview

In order for you to succeed, you will need to adopt good managing skills this year. In any endeavour or decision you wish to partake, outline a plan of action in detail. Consider all your options with scrutiny so that you will take everything into account. Additionally, make the necessary preparations to work with other people as you might find yourself in a partnership sometime soon.

 Wealth

Overall, your outlook on wealth isn't good or bad. For any real change to happen, you really have to put in effort. Your hard work won't immediately see result, instead it will set you up for future gains. This can only be guaranteed if you made your plans prior for the long run.

 Relationships

Romance is in store for single men this year as they may meet the right partner. However, be wary as the new relationship might be threatened immediately from outside influence. For single women, it would be more auspicious to look for love in spring.

 Health

In terms of health, your health will average this year especially for those born in autumn or winter. Some issues related to the stomach might appear such as constipation and haemorrhoids. If any symptoms appear, take them seriously and go for a medical check-up with haste.

 Career

There will be a significant progress and success for your career this year provided you have what it takes to tackle the workload and devote your time. In all likelihood this would exhaust you. On top of that, most of the work that you do will seemingly be unrewarded at first. If you stay determined, the pay out will be worth it.

農曆正月

(February 4th - March 5th) 丙寅
If you're still living with your family, this month you will find yourself feeling dejected with your life.

農曆二月

(March 6th - April 4th) 丁卯
This month, you are more prone to overthinking. Try to see where you are in the real world and plan to act accordingly.

農曆三月

(April 5th - May 5th) 戊辰
Outside forces may try to affect your life at home and work this month. Pay them no attention and stay focused on your goals.

農曆四月

(May 6th - June 5th) 己巳
Arguments will be frequent for married couples this month. Do your best to be more understanding towards your partner and compromise on disagreements.

農曆五月

(June 6th - July 6th) 庚午
If you wait passively, you won't be able to take up any opportunity even if they present themselves. The time to act is now. Do what it takes to realize your goals.

農曆六月

(July 7th - August 7th) 辛未
You might be inclined to keep things to yourself but try practicing honesty this month and open yourself to others. No man is an island.

農曆七月

(August 8th - September 7th) 壬申
In the pursuit of wealth, don't let yourself get blinded by greed. Otherwise, the temptation to take shortcuts through questionable methods might arise.

農曆八月

(September 8th - October 7th) 癸酉
Think all your decisions through before acting on them. Don't decide impulsive just for the sake of getting things done. If you are uncertain with your options, decide on them on a later date.

農曆九月

(October 8th - November 7th) 甲戌
You might advance your career this month in the form of a promotion. Make sure to complete your due tasks to ensure that you are able to take additional responsibilities.

農曆十月

(November 8th - December 6th) 乙亥
If you feel like travelling this month, south or east will bring you good luck.

農曆十一月
(December 7th 2019 - January 5th 2020) 丙子
You might be bet with offers that seem too good to be true, but don't be tempted. It's possibly a ploy to take advantage of you.

農曆十二月

(January 6th - February 3rd 2020) 丁丑
Be wary this month with who you share your ideas with. There are some people around you who are not above taking credit for your effort.

癸卯 Gui Mao Day

Overview

Great results can be expected should you collaborate with others this year such as through partnerships. Any task and goal that you have to complete will be easier to achieve through cooperation and teamwork with your colleagues. While you can be independent, you should be open to the option of relying on others as much as you can to get the work done.

 ## Wealth

Your social network will provide you with wealth opportunities so pay attention to what those around you have to say. Any opinion or advice they have might end up being a crucial piece of information that would be beneficial for you.

 ## Relationships

There's a possibility that the person you're attracted to is somehow connected to your friends. For those in a relationship, some instabilities may lie ahead and as such you have to put in the effort to resolve it. Trust issues may also arise so honest communication should be applied.

 ## Health

Overall your health would be good this year. If you are over thirty years old however, your cholesterol levels might rise possibly caused by your sugar consumption. Practice moderation when it comes to sweets and go for regular medical examinations to prevent worse problems.

 ## Career

It would be highly beneficial for your career this year if you play on the social aspect. Even if you are an introvert, you can still benefit through your pre-existing social network. On the downside, you're also susceptible to rumours and gossip. Whatever you have to share with others, have some wisdom in who you tell it to and what you tell them.

農曆正月

(February 4th - March 5th) 丙寅
Do not be discouraged by apparent favouritism in the office. Be the more mature individual by moving ahead and continuing to do your job. Lend your support to others and be open to their ideas so that you will eventually come to be seen as a valuable part of the workplace.

農曆二月

(March 6th - April 4th) 丁卯
You have a lot of ideas you wish to share and you're going to need someone to listen to them. Try to find anyone who might be able to lend an ear.

農曆三月

(April 5th - May 5th) 戊辰
You might quarrel with people at work this month but it shouldn't be anything damning if you can keep your emotions in check.

農曆四月

(May 6th - June 5th) 己巳
Your hard work and efforts are paying off this month and you may receive a financial gain. Spend what you have wisely to avoid wasting your well-earned labour on trivial expenditure.

農曆五月
(June 6th - July 6th) 庚午
As your stress levels increase, your immunity system will be affected negatively. Find a way to get away from your problems for a moment to recuperate before the symptoms get worse.

農曆六月

(July 7th - August 7th) 辛未
Sarcastic remark might offend the sensitivities of others this month. Think carefully about the things you say or do so it won't be misinterpreted by anyone.

農曆七月

(August 8th - September 7th) 壬申
This month, you may experience an increase in wealth luck, particularly for those born in summer.

農曆八月

(September 8th - October 7th) 癸酉
You may be heading north this month on the pretence of travel. Have an open mind and see how you can take full advantage of this opportunity.

農曆九月

(October 8th - November 7th) 甲戌
There's a person in your life that you are unsatisfied or unhappy with. Whatever problems you have with that person, have a heart-to-heart talk with them with sincerity.

農曆十月

(November 8th - December 6th) 乙亥
In the process of completing your task, you might find yourself being distracted by your colleagues and friends this month. Stay focused on your goals.

農曆十一月
(December 7th 2019 - January 5th 2020) 丙子
You may be able to receive some form of career advancement should you travel southwards this month.

農曆十二月

(January 6th - February 3rd 2020) 丁丑
You might be able to find inspiration from those around you. Good ideas will only come to you should you open yourself up to what they might suggest and show your gratitude.

甲辰 Jia Chen Day

Overview

You may have to overcome some obstacles in your life this year with the help of the people around you. Maintain your bridges with your social circle so that they will be available whenever you need them in any way possible. In terms of wealth, things are not looking so good. At the same time, you should see this as something temporary that will eventually pass and in the meanwhile, plan for your future financial prospects.

 ## Wealth

Overall, your wealth will be fairly ordinary for this year, provided you're careful with your budget. Should you give into impulsive spending, the repercussion would be hard to recover from. In the event that you are unable to resist the temptation to spend money, at the very least spend it on investments or opportunities that will help you earn more in the long run.

 ## Relationships

Things are not looking good for relationships in general for you. If you're in a relationship, there will be constant arguments that would test your patience. If you're single, you'll probably stay single even so it's best that you take this year to focus on improving other aspects of yourself besides your love life.

 ## Health

Go for regular check-ups this year as you might encounter issue with your kidneys and blood pressure. It would also help to supplement with a healthier diet and exercise. If any symptoms become apparent, seek immediate medical attention before it gets worse. Skin problems and allergies might also occur, especially for those born in summer.

 ## Career

You might be going through a career change sometime this year. Make the necessary preparations so that when the time comes, you'll be ready to excel in a new environment. Seeking partnerships is recommended to ensure some sense of security and efficiency in your endeavour. This will result in significant success in your career.

農曆正月

(February 4th - March 5th) 丙寅
You might be prone to emotional outbursts this month. With that in mind, go for diplomatic options when it comes to disputes.

農曆二月

(March 6th - April 4th) 丁卯
This month, you may face additional competition at work. Do what is necessary to prepare yourself in handling them. Also, you might experience fever and sore throats.

農曆三月

(April 5th - May 5th) 戊辰
You might feel that this month would be tiring for you and as a result your motivation would suffer. Don't let it get the best of you and remain focused to get your work done.

農曆四月

(May 6th - June 5th) 己巳
If you ever need help, remember that your friends are there for you. Try to seek the opinion of others before coming to conclusion with any decision as they will help you to pick the best choice.

農曆五月

(June 6th - July 6th) 庚午
If you have a project going on, you may need some extra funding for it. If so, go ahead and ask for financial aid. Be ready to face such a scenario and plan accordingly.

農曆六月

(July 7th - August 7th) 辛未
This month, you may see better financial rewards at work.

農曆七月

(August 8th - September 7th) 壬申
You may see plenty of new chances for financial gain this month that comes with you in a position of power and authority. However, this can only

happen once you earned it to deserve the trust and respect required of the role.

農曆八月

(September 8th - October 7th) 癸酉
Just because you're impatient, don't act too hastily. Any shortcuts that you take this month will do more bad than good so curb your impulses. The easy way might see tempting in the short term but hard work and patience will provide better results in the future.

農曆九月

(October 8th - November 7th) 甲戌
It will be an inspirational month for you are able to general innovative ideas easily. These ideas can be implemented in practice only if you do the required work for them. Otherwise, they'll remain as daydream.

農曆十月

(November 8th - December 6th) 乙亥
Your superiors will finally notice your talents and effort this month. You will be rewarded for your work with praises and you'll gain the recognition for them.

農曆十一月

(December 7th 2019 - January 5th 2020) 丙子
If you're in a relationship, expect disagreements with your partner constantly throughout this month. If it goes on, it might even spell the end of it. Try to be the better person in the relationship and always go for compromise. Whatever problems you have, it's important to solve them rather than escalating the matter.

農曆十二月

(January 6th - February 3rd 2020) 丁丑
Practice some restrain in your speech for this month. You might feel like saying some cutting things once in a while, but don't. Nothing good will come out of it.

乙巳 Yi Si Day

Overview

It's a good year to be in the creative industry for you as your inspiration is set to flourish. You will find many opportunities that would allow your talents to shine. Make the necessary preparations so you would be ready to make full use of these chances. At the same time, your financial state this year needs caution as it stands on uneven ground.

 Wealth

For the first half of the year, there will be plenty of opportunities to expand your wealth. Once it is obtained, make sure you handle it wisely. Should you spend it unnecessarily and impulsively, it will set you back in the long run.

 Relationships

In terms of love and romance, it won't be a good year for you. If you are single and looking, what you will find is likely to be rejection or lack of chemistry. Don't worry too much about it as you can see this as an opportunity to focus on improving other aspects of your life. The right time will come eventually where you will meet the right person for you.

 Health

This year will be quite emotionally taxing for you. As such, learn how to handle your stress and anger in a productive manner. If you let it get the best of you, it may manifest itself as physical health problems. Keep your professional and personal life separate in order to ensure that they won't affect each other negatively.

 Career

Rather than waiting for opportunities to present itself to you, you should be proactive in looking for them. Many of the opportunities out there are up for grabs only if you are able to seek them. Perhaps you can learn new skills and diversify your talents that would increase the value of what you are able to contribute.

農曆正月

(February 4th - March 5th) 丙寅
This month, you may expect changes that are positive in nature at your workplace. It may be a salary boost or a brand-new boss.

農曆二月

(March 6th - April 4th) 丁卯
A stressful month can be expected with an increase in workflow, and this is particular true for those born during summer. You should be smart in scheduling your timetable so you would not succumb to stress stemming from overworking.

農曆三月

(April 5th - May 5th) 戊辰
You would be able to complete your tasks if you put your mind to it. Believe in your own ability to deliver and you will be able to create substantial progress.

農曆四月

(May 6th - June 5th) 己巳
This month, you might be riddled with decisions you are unsure of. In that regard, you may want to get the opinion of others to ease you into making the right choices.

農曆五月

(June 6th - July 6th) 庚午
A challenging month can be expected stemming from your competition. Be prepared for them with intuitive strategy and planning. This would be an opportunity for you to learn from the experience and better equip yourself for future conflicts.

農曆六月

(July 7th - August 7th) 辛未
This month, you may find yourself at disagreements in your workplace. Instead of letting it fester, take the problem head on with diplomacy and handle it with minimal interference from your emotions.

農曆七月

(August 8th - September 7th) 壬申
You may expect positive changes in your life this month. Getting out of your comfort zone and adapting to these changes would be favourable for you.

農曆八月

(September 8th - October 7th) 癸酉
As there is a risk of robbery this month, make sure you keep your personal items as well as yourself safe. Seeming random mood swings can also be expected.

農曆九月

(October 8th - November 7th) 甲戌
Your health might take a hit in the form of respiratory issues, possibly difficulty in breath. Take preventive measures to keep your lung healthy by avoiding any reason that might harm them. Go for a check-up as soon as the symptoms appear.

農曆十月

(November 8th - December 6th) 乙亥
It would be favourable for you to travel for work-related reasons this month. Make the best out of this opportunity and see what you can learn out of it.

農曆十一月

(December 7th 2019 - January 5th 2020) 丙子
This month, you may expect a form of career advancement at work. However, your colleagues might be jealous of your success. Keep a healthy distance between yourself and the petty people who are unable to be happy for you.

農曆十二月

(January 6th - February 3rd 2020) 丁丑
Loneliness would be upon you this month and this may be caused by focusing too much on work and not enough on your relationships. Remember those who are close to you and give them more of your attention.

丙午 Bing Wu Day

Bing

Wu

Overview

If you persevere and do what it takes to move forward, success is secured for you this year. There's a chance that your work will grant you opportunities to travel and should you accept it, it's likely to be beneficial for you. Take this chance to be more proactive and gain recognition and respect at work. You might feel like procrastinating and get yourself distracted but try to remain focused as earning the reward requires effort on your part.

 ## Wealth

This year, your finances are not steady. Consider long-term investments for your savings as opposed to frivolous spending as your budget is quite tight. Be more prudent with your finances and plan it wisely to ensure you make the best out of it.

 ## Relationships

For those in relationships, it will be a troubling year. Before problems escalate into drastic outcomes, married couples should settle their problems with one another as quickly as they could. For the most part, a big part of your schedule would be devoted to solving relationship issues. Try your best in your own way to handle your personal problems and at the same time not let it affect the other things in your life.

 ## Health

Aside from blood pressure and stomach related issues, you should be fine this year. Consider eating healthier and get yourself checked regularly. Your weight might cause you more problems down the line so it would be wise if you can keep it under control.

 ## Career

Focus on your work and try not to give in to procrastination. Keep going with the hard work, give out ideas and whenever you're given the chance to travel, take it. These will help you career-wise and takes you closer to realizing your ambitions. If you keep up with bad habits instead, it would lead you to stagnation.

農曆正月

(February 4th - March 5th) 丙寅
In terms of finance, it's a good month for you as you might see a good amount of profit and wealth opportunities.

農曆二月

(March 6th - April 4th) 丁卯
Great opportunities for success is for you this month through networking. You will find yourself with people who are able to give you useful advice and show you the right direction to take.

農曆三月

(April 5th - May 5th) 戊辰
You might be the recipient for a promotion this month and this is especially true for those born in autumn or winter. Don't take too long to think about or else you might just miss out on this opportunity.

農曆四月

(May 6th - June 5th) 己巳
Minimize your interactions as your emotions are unstable this month. You might reach a boiling point and blow up if you're not too careful with it.

農曆五月

(June 6th - July 6th) 庚午
Your skills and knowledge will prove to be financially useful as there are people willing to pay you for them.

農曆六月

(July 7th - August 7th) 辛未
This month, you would be feeling more lethargic than usual with your energy level constantly depleted and your immune system at risk.

農曆七月

(August 8th - September 7th) 壬申
When it comes to your own work, it is up to you to complete it despite help from your friends. Focus on getting it done and continue with your hard work.

農曆八月

(September 8th - October 7th) 癸酉
Your Peach Blossom Luck is strong this month so it's a good time for romance. Don't be scared to go out and mingle and put yourself in the position where you can meet new people.

農曆九月

(October 8th - November 7th) 甲戌
At work, you might begin to see some changes that aren't beneficial to you. Take this as an opportunity to learn and grow. At the same time, focus on more important tasks at hand.

農曆十月

(November 8th - December 6th) 乙亥
In this month, travellers are recommended to head south. It is also a good time for teamwork.

農曆十一月

(December 7th 2019 - January 5th 2020) 丙子
You might face some health issues this month caused by food allergies. Your emotions are also prone to mood-swings and irritation so try to look after your well-being physically and mentally better.

農曆十二月

(January 6th - February 3rd 2020) 丁丑
Those who are married will have to deal with disputes. Try to be patient with your significant other and compromise on debated issues so that these sorts of problems don't escalate.

丁未 Ding Wei Day

Overview

You will find this year to be especially tiring and busy. This would likely lead to stress and at the same time, some of it would come from your family as well. Therefore, it is important at times to step back, unwind and relax to get yourself back on your feet. Once you make it through the tough times, you will make easy progress.

 ### Wealth

As your wealth luck is unfavourable for this year, be mindful of your financial spending. Make sure to keep track of your budget and plan ahead in order to avoid over-spending. If you are born in the summer, however, this effect is less pronounced.

 ### Relationships

If you're considering to settle down and start a family, this would be an ideal year for you. But should you decide to do so, you must be clear of mind and ready to compromise. Take into consideration the concerns and needs of others. Married women in particular need to watch out for potential problems.

 ### Health

This would be a good time for you to take note of what food you're consuming and stop eating unhealthily, especially if you were born in winter. After ridding yourself of junk food, perhaps you could go on detox in order to cleanse your system; allowing yourself to have a fresh start. This will definitely help in curbing your bad habits in the long run.

 ### Career

If you focus on your career goals this year, your effort will be rewarded. As long as you can ignore distractions, productivity and progress will be gained quickly. You might even get a job promotion if you remain committed to your goals.

農曆正月

(February 4th - March 5th) 丙寅
For this month, your financial outlook is positive. It's a chance for you to take one or two additional sources of income.

農曆二月

(March 6th - April 4th) 丁卯
You will find that your previous month luck would continue. As such, it would be wise to make full use of any opportunities that you receive.

農曆三月

(April 5th - May 5th) 戊辰
Communication will be a difficulty for you in this month. This will lead to unstable relationships, especially with your superiors at work. Try your best to make sure whatever it is you're trying to say is understood to prevent misunderstanding.

農曆四月

(May 6th - June 5th) 己巳
Keep an eye out for any legal issue that might appear this month. If you don't settle them immediately, it might grow worse and cause you worse problems in the future.

農曆五月

(June 6th - July 6th) 庚午
Be open to the advice and opinion from those around you. You will find support and people who are receptive of your ideas and they will gladly offer you assistance with them.

農曆六月

(July 7th - August 7th) 辛未
As you are more susceptible to food poisoning this month, lookout on what and where you eat. Make sure the food that you eat is hygienic.

農曆七月

(August 8th - September 7th) 壬申
In this month, it is likely your spouse may do something that would upset you. You should however keep your emotions in check in order to keep the problems at a minimum.

農曆八月

(September 8th - October 7th) 癸酉
Pay attention to the details of legal documents this month, especially ones that require a signature. Read exactly what it says before you commit as you might find yourself in trouble over a tiny detail that you could miss out.

農曆九月

(October 8th - November 7th) 甲戌
You will find yourself calmer as this is a month of clarity and balance. As self-awareness will come to you naturally, it's a good time to re-examine yourself to find your own faults and flaws in order to make some self-improvement.

農曆十月

(November 8th - December 6th) 乙亥
As it is not a good month to be spontaneous, don't give into your impulses. Before you say or do anything, think carefully as every action has consequences.

農曆十一月

(December 7th 2019 - January 5th 2020) 丙子
You may be tempted to make some quick cash by ignoring the rules, but it's not worth it. The consequences will be heavy if you do not refrain yourself from taking the improper way to wealth.

農曆十二月

(January 6th - February 3rd 2020) 丁丑
For married men, they will be tied down at work with a busy schedule that takes them away from their family, making it a difficult month for them. The needs of their families would only add on more pressure to them.

戊申 Wu Shen Day

Overview

Your luck would be only moderate this year. However, it will also be mostly positive. Your opportunities for wealth would mostly be derived from travelling as these opportunities would allow you to expand your networks. If you were born during autumn or winter season, your top priority should be your health this year.

 ## Wealth

Your efforts in expanding your wealth is likely to bear fruit this year. Investments made in the past would also be paying off. As your wealth increases, don't let it compromise your work ethic and maintain the momentum to continue rising. For business owners, you may want to consider new markets to expand your business regardless of geographical limitations.

 ## Relationships

For men who are still single, they will experience positive Peach Blossom Luck. This would allow them to possibly meet someone special. Married men however might get entangled with some minor flirtations with third-party which might damage their marriage. For single women, they would also enjoy good Peach Blossom Luck.

 ## Health

If you were born during autumn or winter season, your health is top priority. You may be afflicted with some minor issues regarding your stomach and other gastrointestinal organs such as the liver but nothing serious. You are also at risk to injure your limbs especially on your right side.

 ## Career

You may expect substantial advancement in your career this year. You will find business-related travels hand-in-hand with promotions. If you consider to change jobs, you will find that there would be a lot of offers for you. Before you make any decision, though, think them through.

農曆正月

(February 4th - March 5th) 丙寅
Expect some rivalry at work this month. Take this as a challenge and opportunity. Collaboration with trusted colleagues will be beneficial for everyone involved.

農曆二月

(March 6th - April 4th) 丁卯
Your wealth luck might be positive this month, but minor health issues would prove to be distraction. Solve your health problems before you settle your money worries.

農曆三月

(April 5th - May 5th) 戊辰
If you were born in summer or autumn season, your luck would be great when it comes to teamwork for collaborative projects and group work.

農曆四月

(May 6th - June 5th) 己巳
Practice restrain when it comes to your spending this month. Short-term investments that are seemingly too good to be true must be avoided especially for those born in autumn.

農曆五月

(June 6th - July 6th) 庚午
This month, you might find yourself to be promoted. Set aside some time for you to celebrate as you would need to prepare for your new set of responsibilities.

農曆六月

(July 7th - August 7th) 辛未
On the road, be cautious as there is a possibility of accidents or law-related troubles.

農曆七月

(August 8th - September 7th) 壬申
If there's any new skill that you've always wanted to learn, this would be a good month to acquire them and obtain new experiences.

農曆八月

(September 8th - October 7th) 癸酉
For those who are single, this month would be a good Peach Blossom Luck. It's a good time to be assertive when it comes to romance as the outcome would be favourable.

農曆九月

(October 8th - November 7th) 甲戌
At work, you can achieve much more and get a lot of things done if you are willing to collaborate with your colleagues.

農曆十月

(November 8th - December 6th) 乙亥
Your emotions are unbalanced this month and this would lead to disagreements. Your ego might tell you otherwise but learn to put others first to settle any issues that you have.

農曆十一月

(December 7th 2019 - January 5th 2020) 丙子
When it comes to planning, make sure you have done so thoroughly that there are no loopholes that might cause the whole thing to collapse on itself. Be adaptable to any changes and open yourself to criticism.

農曆十二月

(January 6th - February 3rd 2020) 丁丑
For those who are in relationships, they would be arguing over financial related issues. Don't let your emotions get the best of you and don't let these problems grow out of propotion.

己酉 Ji You Day

己
Ji

酉
You

Overview

In this year, the plans you wish to accomplish will able to be done without much problem. This momentum will contribute to building your confidence in yourself. What's more is that your wealth luck is looking great as well so your finances are secured. Since you are in a position where you are stable and steadily rising, it would be imperative for you to avoid any financial pitfalls such as risky investments or gambling. Your best bet at the moment would be to strategize for the future and handle your budget tightly.

 ## Wealth

Throughout the year, your wealth luck would remain strong. Perhaps you would find an increment in your salary. For entrepreneurs and business owners, consider stepping up your game by expanding your market beyond the borders. Try and see if you can find the opportunities in foreign lands. As you will receive help from many parties that are interested, it shouldn't be a problem.

 ## Relationships

For those who are already in a long-term relationship, consider making it official this year. If you are a single woman, you might have a couple of individuals who are interested in you at the moment. For married women, there are possible temptations that might harm your marriage and arguments regarding money is to be expected.

 ## Health

Overall, your physical health should be okay this year without much issue. But, it's important to practice a healthy living style. Practice moderation when it comes to what you eat, exercise regularly, go for a medical check-up every now and then and you'll be fine. Good health is something almost everyone takes for granted and it's better to prevent than it is to cure any ailment.

 ## Career

In terms of career, this year seems to be quite promising. You may get the chance to travel and along with it are opportunities for you to advance in your career. The rewards that can be gain will come in both financial and reputation boon. Don't hesitate when the opportunities present themselves as the results would be positive.

農曆正月

(February 4th - March 5th) 丙寅
If you see any investment that seems too good to be true, avoid it. Risky investments and dodgy business proposals may be a farce to cheat you out of your money, particularly for those who own businesses or in a partnership.

農曆二月

(March 6th - April 4th) 丁卯
Jealousy and rivalry from other people would escalate this month. This animosity would stem from the fact that you are being acknowledged for your skills and talent.

農曆三月

(April 5th - May 5th) 戊辰
It's time for your investment to pay off this month. For the time being, keep the profits for yourself instead of immediately putting it back into investment as it is not an auspicious time to do so.

農曆四月

(May 6th - June 5th) 己巳
You might be feeling stressed from work, more so than usual, so consider doing activities that could alleviate your worries.

農曆五月

(June 6th - July 6th) 庚午
Health issues, including physical injuries, may arise this month for you especially around the head area. It may be headaches or migraines.

農曆六月

(July 7th - August 7th) 辛未
Doing the same thing over and over again might be a waste of your time, so try to be innovative and take fresh new approaches in how you go about things.

農曆七月

(August 8th - September 7th) 壬申
Remember your goals and do what you have to do to achieve them. Being determined and focused would make you more productive overall.

農曆八月

(September 8th - October 7th) 癸酉
This month can be emotionally tiring for you. There's no shame in seeking support from family and friends whenever your feelings get a bit too much.

農曆九月

(October 8th - November 7th) 甲戌
Try to keep a low profile this month at your workplace. This is to avoid you from getting caught in some petty drama that would distract you from your work.

農曆十月

(November 8th - December 6th) 乙亥
If those close to you need your help, be generous and do what you can for them. At the same time, remember to do it within your reasonable limits and not let yourself become a doormat.

農曆十一月

(December 7th 2019 - January 5th 2020) 丙子
You might be tempted to buy things you don't need on impulse this month. Don't waste your hard-earned money on them and it's better for you to save up instead.

農曆十二月

(January 6th - February 3rd 2020) 丁丑
Starting a new business or going for a new investment would not be favourable this month. The results gained for the time being would not being positive.

庚戌 **Geng Xu Day**

Overview

In order for you to be successful this year, you need to work on it; especially if the work needed is under strict deadlines and inflexible procedures. You may also be travelling abroad for work should you accept the task. Anywhere you go in your life, make sure you practice diplomacy and professionalism with everyone you meet. If you are a student, you may expect yourself to do well in your examinations.

 ## Wealth

You might be spending more than you earn this year so be frugal with your budget. Unnecessary expenditures may bring you temporary happiness but, in the end, they would only put a dent in your finances. Discipline is key in handling your money. When it comes to investments, go for the ones that are risk-free and short-term.

 ## Relationships

Your friends might try to meddle with the romantic aspect of your life for one reason or another, but ultimately it would be detrimental for your relationship. Try to prevent their interference. Women in general will have better luck when it comes to relationships. For those who are married, they should have faith in their intuition rather than the hearsay of others.

 ## Health

Overall, this year your health would be mediocre. Some ear related issue can be expected so go for medical treatment when the symptom arises. Issues regarding your blood pressure may also appear if you are around thirty-five years old or older. Don't wait until it gets worse, seek medical treatment the soonest you can.

 ## Career

Those who are in the education industry will find this year to be auspicious in terms of their career as promotion may be in the bag. For those in other industries, some strategy and planning are required if you wish to gain positive results. You might unintentionally offend others with what you say or do so be careful with how you present yourself and keep your emotions in check.

農曆正月

(February 4th - March 5th) 丙寅
Your wealth luck is looking good this month. Be more assertive in looking for opportunities that would allow you to gain additional income.

農曆二月

(March 6th - April 4th) 丁卯
If you were born during summer, you might be plagued with minor health issues such as fevers or sore throat this month.

農曆三月

(April 5th - May 5th) 戊辰
If you were born during winter, you will be able to find success at work as you may advance in your career this month.

農曆四月

(May 6th - June 5th) 己巳
This month, the workload that you have might seem daunting to take on. The increased workload wouldn't be as scary if you could get it done one at a time.

農曆五月

(June 6th - July 6th) 庚午
You might be inspired this month with creative ways to expand your wealth in the form of side income.

農曆六月

(July 7th - August 7th) 辛未
A busy month can be expected this time of year. Through your teamwork with others, you should be able to get through this month just fine.

農曆七月

(August 8th - September 7th) 壬申
You should be careful with the people around you and what you say to them. There's a possibility that your ideas might get stolen if you are not too careful.

農曆八月

(September 8th - October 7th) 癸酉
Safety should be a concern for pregnant women this month. For everyone else, they may get injured on their right limb.

農曆九月

(October 8th - November 7th) 甲戌
This month, you may find the motivation to change certain things with your life. Take this opportunity to enact the necessary changes that would increase your quality of life.

農曆十月

(November 8th - December 6th) 乙亥
Any endeavour that is deemed risky should be avoided this month. Take the time instead to formulate strategies for the future in order to avoid any disastrous situations.

農曆十一月

(December 7th 2019 - January 5th 2020) 丙子
You may feel like work is important to you but remember that you have loved ones that require your time an attention as well.

農曆十二月

(January 6th - February 3rd 2020) 丁丑
Your stomach or digestive system might be causing your problems this month. It would be best for you to watch your diet more carefully and practice good hygiene.

辛亥 Xin Hai Day

Overview

You can expect great changes in your life this year. For better or worse, you have to be ready when the time comes. It would be wise to see this as a chance for you to improve for the better and get out of your comfort zone. If you take the initiative to ride the wave of change, it will be favourable. Don't be afraid to adopt new methods to ensure progress in your efforts.

 ## Wealth

In terms of wealth, your efforts may not immediately bear fruit, but stay determined. You should consider taking this opportunity to plan ahead for the future. With great preparation and back up plans, you will be ready for future trials and tribulation.

 ## Relationships

Managing your relationships won't be easy for you this year. For men, you will need to invest more time in your relationship so that your partner won't feel neglected. For women, you might be able to find love at your workplace. However, what you find will not last, therefore it's advisable that you simply focus on your career instead.

 ## Health

For those born in autumn or winter, stomach flu and digestive problems could be expected this year. Besides these issues, you'll be relatively fine. Even so, it wouldn't hurt to make positive changes in how you take care of your health, perhaps by adopting a healthier diet.

 ## Career

Smooth sailing can be expected of your career, though sometimes you will be at odds with your boss due to conflicting personalities. Consider communicating in written format as you are less likely to be misconstrued compared to speech.

農曆正月

(February 4th - March 5th) 丙寅
You may find some trouble brewing at home. Don't think about it too much as it will prove to be distracting if you do.

農曆二月

(March 6th - April 4th) 丁卯
If you need help, your team is there for you so don't be afraid to seek aid from them.

農曆三月

(April 5th - May 5th) 戊辰
This month, some of your work may be delayed. Even so, you should maintain your momentum and remain focused.

農曆四月

(May 6th - June 5th) 己巳
Mind what you say this month as you may unintentionally hurt others with your words.

農曆五月

(June 6th - July 6th) 庚午
There's a chance for you to receive a financial gain this month. Before anything, try to remember those who have helped you to obtain it and don't forget to share your reward with them.

農曆六月

(July 7th - August 7th) 辛未
When it comes to wealth, be more proactive and take an aggressive stance in your pursuit as it would bring you results.

農曆七月

(August 8th - September 7th) 壬申
There is an opportunity for you to travel this month. Should you decide to do so, practice caution on the road as there is a chance for accidents.

農曆八月

(September 8th - October 7th) 癸酉
Don't let ego stand in your way if ever you need help at work. Noble People who are capable and willing to help are always around.

農曆九月

(October 8th - November 7th) 甲戌
This month will allow you to generate more creative ideas and stay motivated.

農曆十月

(November 8th - December 6th) 乙亥
There's a risk of you to lose your money or personal belongs this month so it's wise to keep an eye on them. Be ready for unexpected spending due to medical related reasons as well.

農曆十一月

(December 7th 2019 - January 5th 2020) 丙子
There may be petty people who are looking to bring you down by spreading malicious rumours and gossip. Do your best to avoid them altogether.

農曆十二月

(January 6th - February 3rd 2020) 丁丑
If you were born in autumn or winter, working with others as a team will provide the best results this month.

壬子 **Ren Zi Day**

Overview
This is the year where you will be blessed by luck in terms of professional connection with others. If you're working in an office environment, you are able to form stronger bonds with your colleagues. If you run a business, there are opportunities for you to collaborate or enter into partnerships. Don't be quick to dismiss the importance of teamwork. By being more open to working with others will bring you more opportunities.

 ## Wealth
In terms of wealth, this would be an auspicious year for you. Remember to keep in mind those who have helped you achieve your success. You might also want to go out and find someone that you or your business can work with together in a collaboration.

 ## Relationships
It would be best if you focus more on your work rather than looking for relationships this year. It's not that there isn't anyone who is interested in you, it's just that they will take more than they would give in your relationship with them. If you're already in a relationship, remember to pay attention to your partner as to not leave them feeling neglected.

 ## Health
You might feel like you're fine, but you should always be vigilant with your health especially for those born in winter. Go for regular medical check-ups to make sure that you're okay. Your immune system may be compromised this year so frequent illness will follow suit accompanied by prolonged symptoms.

 ## Career
If you'd like your career to advance this year, the best way to go about it is through teamwork. As such, be more receptive to what those around you can do and consider the things they have to say. If you work for others, it's imperative that you keep yourself in your boss' good grace as they would be vital in ensuring your success.

農曆正月

(February 4th - March 5th) 丙寅
A good month awaits you where your boss will be open to hear your ideas as they will be supportive of you.

農曆二月

(March 6th - April 4th) 丁卯
Your boss would recognize your efforts at work this month and the value that you bring to the organization is acknowledged.

農曆三月

(April 5th - May 5th) 戊辰
Make an effort to include others in your endeavours as collaboration will bring you forward. Listen to what ideas they might have and remember to acknowledge their contribution as well.

農曆四月

(May 6th - June 5th) 己巳
Your stomach might cause you some health issues this month so be extra careful with the things you eat.

農曆五月

(June 6th - July 6th) 庚午
Your mother might suffer from health issues, in turn it will be a hit on your finances due to the resulting medical bill.

農曆六月

(July 7th - August 7th) 辛未
Be careful with what you say as they may potentially hurt others around you. Be sure to keep in mind the sensibility of other people.

農曆七月

(August 8th - September 7th) 壬申
Continue engaging in teamwork and collaboration as you will enjoy good wealth luck this month.

農曆八月

(September 8th - October 7th) 癸酉
In this month, you will feel like you're working your hardest. Even when you're doing your best and it takes a toll on you, you should stay determined.

農曆九月

(October 8th - November 7th) 甲戌
You may expect a promotion for you this month. Be bold enough to go out and ask for it as long as you have worked hard to earn what is yours.

農曆十月

(November 8th - December 6th) 乙亥
Try not to make any big choices when it comes to money this month. Wait for another time that is more auspicious when it comes to major spending.

農曆十一月

(December 7th 2019 - January 5th 2020) 丙子
This month, it would be fruitful for you to expand your social network. It will be instrumental to your success once you've made the connection with the right people.

農曆十二月

(January 6th - February 3rd 2020) 丁丑
The new acquaintances that you have made may provide financial opportunities for you. See what they have to say and consider making them a part of your plans.

癸丑 Gui Chou Day

Overview
Whatever challenge you have to go through this year, take them on directly especially if it is related to money. Put in the necessary effort and at the same time have some wisdom going about it in order to maximize the results. Find new ways to reinvent yourself and your ideas so your progress towards your goals are unhindered.

 ## Wealth
When it comes to wealth, it will be an average year for you. With that in mind, focus on building up your savings or invest in things that would grow in value. For any decision that is related to finances, you need to weight your options carefully and not to make immediate judgement.

 ## Relationships
Your love prospect is not looking very well this year as possibilities of third-party affairs might disrupt your relationship. In dealing with matters of the heart, tread carefully and make sure you don't do anything that you will regret later on.

 ## Health
The many responsibilities you have this year would result in anxiety and in turn, stress. Set aside some time to give yourself a much-needed break. Potentially, your heart and liver might cause you problems as well.

 ## Career
You need to take the amount of effort you put in your work to the next level. Keep your eyes on the prize and focus on completing your tasks. How much you are rewarded will depend on how hard you work. Brave through the initial difficulties to reap the bigger reward later on.

農曆正月

(February 4th - March 5th) 丙寅
You may run into some additional income this month. However, make sure your means are legitimate and ethical.

農曆二月

(March 6th - April 4th) 丁卯
There's a chance you might say or do something offensive this month so be careful with your behaviour.

農曆三月

(April 5th - May 5th) 戊辰
Stay on your path towards achieving your goals and contribute to your own cause by obtaining new skills or experiences.

農曆四月

(May 6th - June 5th) 己巳
Minor health issues might plague you this month. Consider taking the necessary choices to improve your overall health, perhaps by taking care of your diet better.

農曆五月

(June 6th - July 6th) 庚午
This month, you are susceptible to mood swings. Your state of mind could be further affected negatively by arguments at home. Give yourself a break and do some introspection and learn to control your emotions better.

農曆六月

(July 7th - August 7th) 辛未
Those close to you might approach you and ask for aid. Offer only what you can afford to give and decline politely if you are unable to help.

農曆七月

(August 8th - September 7th) 壬申
In the process of getting your tasks done, remain focused. Ensure that your emotions won't compromise your work and you are able to make full use of your talents.

農曆八月

(September 8th - October 7th) 癸酉
Alcohol should be taken with caution this month, particularly if you are in a social setting. Make sure your behaviour and words in public remain proper.

農曆九月

(October 8th - November 7th) 甲戌
This month you can expect to gain returns from side projects and minor investments as you will be experiencing strong Indirect wealth luck.

農曆十月

(November 8th - December 6th) 乙亥
This would not be a good month for you to decide on any financially related matters and you should postpone your decisions to a much more auspicious time.

農曆十一月

(December 7th 2019 - January 5th 2020) 丙子
If you're driving this month, there's a chance you might get speeding tickets. Drive carefully and obey the law.

農曆十二月

(January 6th - February 3rd 2020) 丁丑
Your hard work and contribution will be acknowledged. If you stay on this path without slowing down, you may eventually advance in your career.

甲寅 Jia Yin Day

甲 Jia
寅 Yin

Overview

Slow progress is a sign when you should start practicing your patience and reposition your senses. Positive fruition is tough as your company and work appearance is rather less impressive. As such, you may be upset and worried when faced with these problems, but don't be fret of it as you should work hard to clear away the obstacles while pursuing your dreams. Focus on the main target and dive all your effort to achieve your goals.

 ## Wealth

Wealth fortune is not favouring you this year as you may have risk of losing money if you are not careful enough. The prospects are only average at peak. That being said, utilize your fund and money for education and self-enrichment investments purpose as these will improve you as a human being. Now, persevere until your wealth prospects to rebound and prevent yourself from long commitment investments since they are not favouring you.

 ## Relationships

Married couples shall look for ways to reignite the fire in their relationship to keep the interests between both of you. Remember to show sufficient love and focus to your spouse or partner and constantly look for exciting activities to enjoy the lovely time between two of you. Single individuals shall be contented with their lives and allocate attention on themselves.

 ## Health

A rather stable health doesn't mean you should ignore the gratefulness you have. Instead, continue to arrange for frequent medical check-ups and schedule for appropriate eating and exercise habit. For those that are thirty and above, pay extra attention over your heart area.

Career

Work growth will be facilitated by your own capabilities and value advancement. Therefore, enrol for classes or professional course to sharpen your original skillsets or to build new abilities as this will make you a more competent person at work. Learning is a lifelong process so though you may face issues along the road, they are nothing but hurdles to be leap over for a better life.

農曆正月

(February 4th - March 5th) 丙寅
Your increased workload shall be seen as openings to perform your skills and abilities.

農曆二月

(March 6th - April 4th) 丁卯
Your gradual pressure at work are due to additional jobs and tasks. Now, don't be too harsh on yourself and a take a break in the form of power nap to keep you going.

農曆三月

(April 5th - May 5th) 戊辰
Stay away from unnecessary thoughts as they will plague your mentality and bother you from appropriate decision making.

農曆四月

(May 6th - June 5th) 己巳
Petty individuals may try to drag you into gossips. That being said, negativities like these shall not prevent you from working hard for your goals. Try to avoid them.

農曆五月

(June 6th - July 6th) 庚午
It's okay to ask for help and assistance when you cannot deal with things alone. You might be blessed with help from excellent individuals.

農曆六月

(July 7th - August 7th) 辛未
Stay proactive as it allows you to get things done efficiently. So, refrain yourself from procrastination.

農曆七月

(August 8th - September 7th) 壬申
You will be going through sudden emotion flows this month, to be coupled with moodiness. Never allow these to affect people around you.

農曆八月

(September 8th - October 7th) 癸酉
You are graced with invaluable person in life that will favour you with assistance. Therefore, do not stay away from them for that they will provide timely help when needed.

農曆九月

(October 8th - November 7th) 甲戌
Wealth fortune is on your side this month, this can be seen especially for individuals that are working in team and collaborative tasks.

農曆十月

(November 8th - December 6th) 乙亥
As the stock market isn't favouring you this month, any unwise investment decisions will only fruit financial losses.

農曆十一月
(December 7th 2019 - January 5th 2020) 丙子
There will be opportunities which you will receive certain work growth this month.

農曆十二月

(January 6th - February 3rd 2020) 丁丑
Those who are particularly born in the summer are prone to high expenses on medical fees.

乙卯 **Yi Mao Day**

Overview

When it comes to career and wealth, it won't be smooth sailing for you this year. Just because there's less progress and activities doesn't mean you should lose hope. Instead, it's an opportunity for you to do some self-improvement. As you would have some extra time to spend, you can utilize it by learning a new skill and hone your talents as this will be useful for you in the future.

 ## Wealth

As your wealth luck might not be so positive this year, handle your spending wisely. Have a financial back up plan so you would always have a safety net ready. If you wish to invest, go through your entire strategy in an organised manner within your own means. If all goes well, you wouldn't find yourself in a financially unstable situation.

 ## Relationships

It's a good year to find romance this year if you are still single. For everyone in general, including those already in a relationship, patience would be a virtue to practice. The key to a strong relationship lies in an honest and open communication between two people. It is imperative that whatever you're trying to say is heard and more importantly, understood.

 ## Health

While not perfect, this year you will be mostly happy. Bear in mind however that your stress level may go up so you have to keep that in check. Take some time off every now and then to relax, unwind and recharge your batteries to avoid exhaustion.

Career

In terms of career, you might find this aspect of your life to be in turmoil this year. While it's not a comfortable place to be, you may want to realign your goals to get yourself back on track. This can also be a test to bring out the best of you and discover hidden talents.

農曆正月

(February 4th - March 5th) 丙寅
For this month, your stress levels would increase. At the same time, don't let it get to you that it would affect your life significantly. Take it one step at a time and remain determined.

農曆二月

(March 6th - April 4th) 丁卯
This month, you might find an opportunity for a new job. Don't make any brash decisions as it might backfire in your face if you go with your impulses.

農曆三月

(April 5th - May 5th) 戊辰
If you have any unfinished businesses, this would be a good time to deal with them. Be more assertive and finish up as much of your tasks as possible.

農曆四月

(May 6th - June 5th) 己巳
Remain steadfast in your goals and responsibilities this month. Don't let trivial distractions get in the way of your productivity.

農曆五月

(June 6th - July 6th) 庚午
Your eyes might experience some issues related to your eyes this month. Additionally, try not to borrow your money to anyone for the time being or go out of your way for others.

農曆六月

(July 7th - August 7th) 辛未
Some people might try to use you as a means to their end, but you should remain steadfast and not let yourself get bullied by them.

農曆七月

(August 8th - September 7th) 壬申
Bouts of mood swing will be present in this month. Confusion is to be expected and your emotions would exaggerate how things actually are in the real world.

農曆八月

(September 8th - October 7th) 癸酉
If someone were to ask you to be their guarantor, it's best that you decline such offer as it would be unfavourable for you.

農曆九月

(October 8th - November 7th) 甲戌
You might feel like spending some money this month on trivial expenditures but try not to. Handle your finances wisely, make a budget and keep to that budget.

農曆十月

(November 8th - December 6th) 乙亥
Everything will be okay in the end. If it's not okay, its not the end yet. Have faith that things will always get better.

農曆十一月

(December 7th 2019 - January 5th 2020) 丙子
At work, make sure your goals and tasks are properly completed without any unforeseen loopholes. Whatever you have started, make sure it gets fully done.

農曆十二月

(January 6th - February 3rd 2020) 丁丑
A new boss may show up at work and this is your chance to form a good relationship with that person.

丙辰 **Bing Chen Day**

丙 Bing 辰 Chen

Overview

If you ever feel like changing your life, this might just be the year to do so. It's the ideal time to get yourself out of your comfort zone to try out unfamiliar things. However, do be mindful of the details when it comes to your work even if you're taking a fresh new angle on it. If you wish to improve your life, creativity is what you need to seek in the form of new experiences. Travelling is a good example of this.

 ### Wealth

Your work life shows signs of improvement this year. But in order for these good changes to happen, you have to initiate it by breaking the same old bad habits. Be more diligent, show more initiative, deal with problems right away and you will find that wealth is ensured for you this year.

 ### Relationships

Peach Blossom Luck is around this year for single women to enjoy. For those who are married on the other hand, they'll find the whole affair to be more boring than it used to be; and this could threaten the marriage. Do something or go somewhere new with your spouse to bring back excitement into your relationship.

 ### Health

You're likely to suffer from migraines and headaches this year that stems from stress. At the same, you're susceptible to head-related injuries as well so it pays to play it safe. Besides these things, your overall health shouldn't give you any issue this year.

 ### Career

Career-wise, you might be moving up on the ladder. Be disciplined with your goals and you will be able to accomplish task after task with great ease. It will be advantageous for you to travel, so take any opportunity to do so whenever they appear.

農曆正月

(February 4th - March 5th) 丙寅
Be confident as this is the month for you to show off your talents and leave good impressions. As long as you're not afraid, you can do it.

農曆二月

(March 6th - April 4th) 丁卯
This month, your wealth luck is looking good. For single men, love is in the air as romantic opportunities are abound.

農曆三月

(April 5th - May 5th) 戊辰
While your career may advance this month, it will be quite stressful. This may cause a strain your relationship.

農曆四月

(May 6th - June 5th) 己巳
It's a good time for you to do a health check-up, just in case you might have any heart-related health issues. Can't be too careful, after all.

農曆五月

(June 6th - July 6th) 庚午
It will be an inspirational month for you as ideas will flow through you like water. Feel free to share these ideas of yours so that they may be useful for you.

農曆六月

(July 7th - August 7th) 辛未
Suspicion and insecurity rules over your relationships this month. Practice honesty and sincerity when it comes to communicating about your feelings and avoid making baseless assumptions.

農曆七月

(August 8th - September 7th) 壬申
Your emotions run wild this month and it can only be calmed by means of travel, specifically towards south.

農曆八月

(September 8th - October 7th) 癸酉
This month, your wealth outlook is looking great, this is especially true for those born in spring or summer. The best outcome of this is achievable through teamwork.

農曆九月

(October 8th - November 7th) 甲戌
You might feel like your hard work is being unnoticed and your boss doesn't appreciate you as much as they should. However, be mindful of your emotions so that it would not aggravate the matter.

農曆十月

(November 8th - December 6th) 乙亥
Your emotional turbulence continues this month. Knowing this, practice professionalism and keep it under control.

農曆十一月

(December 7th 2019 - January 5th 2020) 丙子
This month, you will enjoy good wealth luck as well as encouragement and support in your workplace.

農曆十二月

(January 6th - February 3rd 2020) 丁丑
You might get food poisoning this month so try to scrutinize on what you eat.

丁巳 Ding Si Day

Overview

All the effort that you put in the past will be rewarded as you will be enjoying a fantastic year. Don't be afraid to take on any opportunities that appear before you as your wealth luck would be generally promising. Having said that, make sure to take full advantage of this year by being receptive to more options in order to make progress.

 ## Wealth

When opportunity come knocking on your door, you won't be able to reap the benefit if you don't go ahead and answer it. Be proactive to make the most out of them. There might be a disagreement over finances if you are in a partnership, try to make sure this doesn't escalate.

 ## Relationships

For men who are married, there might be a temptation to be involved in extra-marital affair. Unless you stay faithful in your marriage, it will likely spell the end of it. Always remember to do the right thing and stay true to your duties and obligations. For those who are unmarried, this is a good year for you to tie the knot.

 ## Health

If you were born in summer or autumn, you will have moderate health this year. As there are possibilities of headaches and migraine, remember to take extra precautions with your physical wellbeing.

 ## Career

For those who were born in spring, you can expect advancement in your career or a promotion. However, it won't happen unless you put the right effort into it. You will see better results as long as you keep up with your good work.

農曆正月

(February 4th - March 5th) 丙寅

Be mindful of your head as it is susceptible to injury this month. If there are people in your life that lacks commitment to you and your relationship with them, don't be afraid to part from them.

農曆二月

(March 6th - April 4th) 丁卯

You may be pressured by your colleagues to make hard choices. Do not decide too hastily just because you want them to go away.

農曆三月

(April 5th - May 5th) 戊辰

There's a possibility that you will find a surprise financial windfall this month as the result of your hard work recently. As you've earned it, do not worry about taking some time off.

農曆四月

(May 6th - June 5th) 己巳

Pay attention to the work you submit to make sure that it's presentable and acceptable to your superiors. Make sure to cover all angles so you may not disappoint or be scolded.

農曆五月

(June 6th - July 6th) 庚午

Old legal issues might rear its ugly head once again and now is the time to have it settled for good. Proceed with caution as you don't want your problems to multiply, for example settle your bills on time.

農曆六月

(July 7th - August 7th) 辛未

Your stomach might cause you some issues this month so be mindful of what you eat. Avoid anything that looks like it might upset your stomach and stay hygienic.

農曆七月

(August 8th - September 7th) 壬申

On this month, there's a possibility for you to experience health problems especially around your head area. It may be caused by carelessness on your part, perhaps letting yourself get distracted which caused you to accidentally hurt yourself. As for those born in summer, your legs might get injured.

農曆八月

(September 8th - October 7th) 癸酉

Consider taking on additional training when it comes to work so you're better equipped to handle new projects that might come this month.

農曆九月

(October 8th - November 7th) 甲戌

It is likely that this will be a challenging and annoying month for you as you may find yourself at odds with certain colleagues. Don't let yourself be bullied and be pickier on who you'd put your trust in.

農曆十月

(November 8th - December 6th) 乙亥

On this month, get your eyes checked as it may cause you some problems. Go to the doctor as soon as possible so that you may identify whatever problem you might have whether apparent or not.

農曆十一月

(December 7th 2019 - January 5th 2020) 丙子

There is a possibility for you to travel this month. When you do travel, keep an eye out on your spending as you may overstep your budget. At the same time, be vigilant for your possessions and personal documents.

農曆十二月

(January 6th - February 3rd 2020) 丁丑

You might be feeling like procrastinating but avoid doing so as to avoid the workload from accumulating unnecessarily. Practice discipline and work on your tasks whenever you're free.

戊午 Wu Wu Day

Overview

Your health outlook is looking better this year. You will also find Noble People who will be there to assist you in your activities. Through their help, you would be able to discipline yourself better as there are many opportunities that require the opinion of others especially if they are financially related. It's also a good year to give up on bad habits and adopt new better ones that would be beneficial for you in the long-term.

 ## Wealth

There are many ways to create wealth and should you utilize your creativity with innovation and bravery, you will be rewarded for your ingenuity. For those in partnerships, careful with what and how you communicate as you might misunderstand each other. You might also have to settle for less, but at the same time you should be appreciative towards any opportunities that are given anyway. By having this mentality, it will be better for you overall.

 ## Relationships

Good romantic luck awaits single men this year. For women in relationships, they might run into some conflict with their parts. They might also deal with additional problem concerning their partner and an old friend. Handle with care when it comes to these sorts of issues and try to be understanding, compromising and compassionate.

 ## Health

If you were born in spring, your health will be in top shape this year. For everyone else, stomach-related issues might crop up. These problems are not a one-time thing either as they may be recurring.

 ## Career

At work, try to keep your head low as you may need to not get yourself caught in any scandals or arguments. While there will be opportunities to let your efforts and talent shine, it's better if you hold yourself back for the time being. Eventually, you will be rewarded with a form of career advancement sometime in June.

農曆正月

(February 4th - March 5th) 丙寅
It's a good time this month for you to go out and try something new. Forming a new partnership is one of them.

農曆二月

(March 6th - April 4th) 丁卯
Your words might cause unintentional offence to others so be careful with your mouth. At the same time, don't jump to conclusion and refrain from making immediate judgements.

農曆三月

(April 5th - May 5th) 戊辰
The stress from your workplace might increase this month thanks to competition. You may still be able to get yourself ahead should you remain focused and stay determined.

農曆四月

(May 6th - June 5th) 己巳
If you are travelling this month, practice some caution as you may run into an accident. If you allow yourself to be distracted, you might find your safety to be compromised.

農曆五月

(June 6th - July 6th) 庚午
For all your efforts, you might be rewarded with some form of promotion this month. All your hard work, patience and talent is finally bearing fruit.

農曆六月

(July 7th - August 7th) 辛未
Be careful with your surroundings and activities in order to avoid any legal troubles this month. Don't be involved in the problems of others and don't be pressured to get involved either as you will find it to be a waste of your time.

農曆七月

(August 8th - September 7th) 壬申
In terms of financial investments, it's not really a good time. The market as it is at the moment Is rather unstable and any investment you put in would not be beneficial for you.

農曆八月

(September 8th - October 7th) 癸酉
Women who are pregnant may find themselves at risk with health issues this month so they should take better care of their well-being.

農曆九月

(October 8th - November 7th) 甲戌
Finance might be the cause of arguments with your significant other. Don't let these disagreements get out of control as it might be a catalyst that would spell the doom of your relationship. If the situation isn't getting any better, don't let your anger get the better of you.

農曆十月

(November 8th - December 6th) 乙亥
You will find yourself surrounded by baseless rumours and gossip. You might even get backstabbed by those you trust or they might spread more lies. Be careful with who you choose to trust and ignore all those petty people.

農曆十一月

(December 7th 2019 - January 5th 2020) 丙子
It is not beneficial for you be project yourself as someone who is uncaring. Behave in a way that you can be seen as someone who is empathic and considerate so people will find you to be reliable.

農曆十二月

(January 6th - February 3rd 2020) 丁丑
Procrastinating won't do you any favour. Do your work properly and make sure you won't be bogged down with backlog in the future.

己未 Ji Wei Day

Overview

It is a crucial year for you in terms of career advancement. In order for you to realise your goals, you need a more proactive approach. The road to success won't be easy as you may find yourself obstructed by petty people who'd rather see you fail. They will do whatever it takes to bring you down including manufacturing baseless lies and rumours.

 ## Wealth

In terms of your finances, it's looking good. However, if you are in a business or partnership you should be careful. It would be more rewarding for you to be assertive in order to make your goals a reality. Wealth and great rewards can be yours through strategic planning and adequate preparation.

 ## Relationships

Peach Blossom Luck is present this year and single men would benefit more from it than women. For those in a long on-going relationship, it's a good time to make it official. For those already in marriage, beware of outside temptations.

 ## Health

For those born in winter or spring, you don't have to worry about your health too much. For those born in summer or autumn, there's a chance for injuries on your head and limbs as well as a possibility for tumours and growth. Go for medical check-ups as soon as the first symptom appear.

 ## Career

It's possible for you to advance in your career if you put your effort in it. Not doing anything or putting your work on hold would obstruct you from taking on the opportunities that come your way. Make sure you get all your work done so you would be in a position where you are able to adapt to any situation.

農曆正月

(February 4th - March 5th) 丙寅
If you were born in spring, you might find yourself in the losing end of competition. You will need to assert yourself more and utilise your talents to make sure you would be able to keep up.

農曆二月

(March 6th - April 4th) 丁卯
This month, support will be there for you. Any endeavour you wish to partake would be helped by your family and friends.

農曆三月

(April 5th - May 5th) 戊辰
An auspicious month can be expected. Make the most out of this by collaborating with others as the reward gained would be greater. Use the wealth gained as investment and your wealth would steadily grow.

農曆四月

(May 6th - June 5th) 己巳
This month may be difficult for you thanks to conflicts with people around you that's money related. It would be wise for you to stay calm to ensure the problem doesn't get worse.

農曆五月

(June 6th - July 6th) 庚午
Some good news can be expected of your career this month. It's possible that this could mean your career would advance in one way or another.

農曆六月

(July 7th - August 7th) 辛未
As pleasant as it might be to stay in your comfort zone, it would not be beneficial for you to stay in stagnation. Should you take a more direct approach to things and allow yourself to be flexible, it would be easier for you to solve your problems.

農曆七月

(August 8th - September 7th) 壬申
For those who are married, it would be best for everyone if you avoid arguing with each other this month. Road accidents are likely for those on the road so be careful, especially with your right leg being at risk.

農曆八月

(September 8th - October 7th) 癸酉
Great ideas will come to you naturally this month. Take this opportunity to find practical applications with these new ideas to make great progress with your work.

農曆九月

(October 8th - November 7th) 甲戌
It's a good month for you to be working with other people. You will find what they have to offer to be inspirational and by pooling your resources together, everyone will reach greater heights.

農曆十月

(November 8th - December 6th) 乙亥
If you are looking for a partnership this month, don't make any official decisions just yet. However, feel free to look through your plans and think about it for now.

農曆十一月

(December 7th 2019 - January 5th 2020) 丙子
Others may notice you more this month and praise you for the innovative ideas that you've made known to them. Don't be afraid to take the credit for yourself as you have earned it.

農曆十二月

(January 6th - February 3rd 2020) 丁丑
Your body might be at risk to injuries this month. It's nothing severe, though you still need to be vigilant especially when it comes to your limbs.

庚申 Geng Shen Day

Overview

A rocky year in terms of career for you is expected. You will come across unscrupulous individuals that will try to bring down your reputation at work due to their lack of abilities and jealousy. Keep a low profile and continue to work hard. Your calmness is crucial to confront the controversies at workplace which might demand you to explain yourself.

 ## Wealth

Others may approach you or enhance their relationships with you as wealth fortune is on your side. Safeguard yourself and stay prepared by just focusing on your own matters and care less about the others. As days passed, fortune will be smoothen gradually especially those who born in spring and summer seasons approaching the second half year.

 ## Relationships

One may not be able to enjoy romantic relationship if one isn't devoted to pour in effort and hard work. Remember, men that are in relationships shall never ignore their partner while pursuing their interests in other areas, else your spouse may look for another source of attention. Furthermore, woman must practice to be more patient in this year to boost their relationship fortune. That being said, the second half of the year will bring better Peach Blossom Luck.

 ## Health

Your health will be one of the primary concerns in this year. That being said, watch out of your eyes, heart and blood pressure. Women are set to encounter gynaecological health issues too. To counter these problems, schedule for frequent medical check-ups for best prevention.

 ## Career

Dive your effort and focus into workplace while keeping a low profile at all times at work. There will be villains lurking around who could channel their ulterior intentions on you. This can be seen in the form of credit robbery over ideas. Be caution with who you trust. Moreover, endeavour to make every task clear and detailed to avoid unnecessary calamity.

農曆正月

(February 4th - March 5th) 丙寅
Villains are lurking around to steal your innovative ideas, contributing to your shaky month at work. Stay alert to your surroundings to avoid credit robbery over your designated plans.

農曆二月

(March 6th - April 4th) 丁卯
Prospective mothers are set to encounter certain health issues this month. Refrain from any risky actions and take extra of yourself. Consult a doctor immediately if you sense any trouble.

農曆三月

(April 5th - May 5th) 戊辰
New inspiration and thoughts are needed to fuel your execution of plans. You may fruit auspicious result and gain favouring lessons through trying new ideas.

農曆四月

(May 6th - June 5th) 己巳
Though wealth fortune is rooting for you this month, be attention and stay alert especially when you are travelling.

農曆五月

(June 6th - July 6th) 庚午
Wealth fortune will take an even auspicious turn this month. Nonetheless, you excellent luck may draw the jealously and anger from the others. Never let these villains to ruin your month and focus more on yourself.

農曆六月

(July 7th - August 7th) 辛未
Men that are in relationships are expected to come across much disputes with their spouse. However, never bring personal emotion just to win this arguments as momentary satisfaction will only bring weakened romance bond.

農曆七月

(August 8th - September 7th) 壬申
Career fortune are smoothen as fruition of your daily effort and contribution. Such auspiciousness can been seen in the form of promotion or increment this month.

農曆八月

(September 8th - October 7th) 癸酉
Try to delay the major life decisions in this period of time, especially on legal matters.

農曆九月

(October 8th - November 7th) 甲戌
New skillsets and capabilities empower us for better opportunities in life. Therefore, try to sign up a course such as language or other professional programme to stay afresh and keep you going.

農曆十月

(November 8th - December 6th) 乙亥
Your itinerary are filled with social events this month. Having said that, one should not indulge oneself into parties as moderation is crucial for life balance.

農曆十一月

(December 7th 2019 - January 5th 2020) 丙子
Your ideas and thoughts may differ to that of your superiors, leading into arguments. However, as these rather heated discussions are meant for professional reasons, you should avoid bringing personal emotion or even talk bad behind the backs of superiors.

農曆十二月

(January 6th - February 3rd 2020) 丁丑
Health problems such as heart issues are your primary concern this month. For those who are forty and above, they should go for early medical check-ups to avoid the problem.

辛酉 Xin You Day

Overview

Your efforts in the past years are beginning to pay off so expect more positivity this year, especially if you work in an office. Keep the momentum going with your hard work to ensure security in your future and impeccable social standing.

 ### Wealth

When it comes to financial matters, it is important for you to be proactive. Take the initiative to venture into things that you may have not considered before. Don't be afraid to utilize your creativity and try new methods in order to obtain interesting results.

 ### Relationships

For those who are in long-term relationships or marriages, you may expect some emotional upheaval. Be very patient with your significant other, because if you were to show your anger it will only make the situation worse. Make sure you don't argue for nothing and always try to go for diplomacy.

 ### Health

You may be susceptible to blood-related illness and skin allergies, so it's imperative for you to go for regular medical check-ups. You should also pay close attention to your diet as you might be vulnerable to stomach and food poisoning issues as well. If you don't handle these problems as they appear, it could worsen in the future. Practice a healthier lifestyle.

 ### Career

Consider applying for new jobs or positions. There's also chance to travel for work-related reasons. Whatever the case, be more open-minded about it and keep your options open. If you're a business owner, pay closer attention to the people in your company as there may be some problem that you have to tackle early on before it escalates.

農曆正月

(February 4th - March 5th) 丙寅
Business owners can expect this month to be difficult as competition is tough. Make appropriate preparations as you may lose some valuable members of your staff.

農曆二月

(March 6th - April 4th) 丁卯
Competition remains strong well into this month, especially if you were born in summer. Go back to the drawing board with your strategies and consider taking innovative steps to one-up your rivals.

農曆三月

(April 5th - May 5th) 戊辰
Avoid impulsive decisions this month and perhaps start to think things through carefully in order to minimize unwanted results.

農曆四月

(May 6th - June 5th) 己巳
If you let stress get the better of you this month, you might symptoms of stress-related skin problems such as rashes or other allergies. Try to take it easy every now and then.

農曆五月

(June 6th - July 6th) 庚午
Positive wealth luck is to be expected this month especially for those born in winter. Make the best out of it, perhaps by asking for a raise if you feel like you deserve one.

農曆六月

(July 7th - August 7th) 辛未
The positive wealth luck from the previous month continues. If you have any ideas that haven't been implemented before, now's a good time to try them out.

農曆七月

(August 8th - September 7th) 壬申
You might be tempted to bend the rules a bit but avoid doing so. It will only spell legal troubles in the future.

農曆八月

(September 8th - October 7th) 癸酉
Those who were born in the autumn or winter will benefit greatly from working in close collaboration with others this month.

農曆九月

(October 8th - November 7th) 甲戌
Those in relationships will have arguments with their partner stemming from trust issues such as jealousy and insecurity.

農曆十月

(November 8th - December 6th) 乙亥
This month, your emotions will be in turmoil. Knowing you're not seeing things clearly, try to have another person's opinion when weighing in your options to ensure the best results.

農曆十一月

(December 7th 2019 - January 5th 2020) 丙子
If you ever consider going for partnerships and joint ventures, now is the right time as the opportunity to do so might appear this month.

農曆十二月

(January 6th - February 3rd 2020) 丁丑
This month will be stressful for you, so handle it with wisdom. Always remember that you're allowed to take breaks in order for you to get yourself back on track.

壬戌 **Ren Xu Day**

Overview

All your hard work will finally pay off for you this year and you may reap the benefits that you richly deserve. Having said that, you shouldn't slow down with your pace as there's much more to be gained. Keep up with the good work and you'll eventually propel yourself to greater heights in the future. Look out for opportunities to work with others this year as teamwork will allow you to advance in your endeavours smoothly.

Wealth

Whenever possible, go for projects and prospects that require collaborations with other people as this would be most efficient. When you're pursuing wealth, do it out of passion rather than focusing on monetary gain as greed will cause you to lose sight of the bigger picture.

Relationships

If you're single, it's a good year for romance. You might be able to meet a potential partner at your workplace or through career-related functions or contacts. You might be disappointed with some of those you meet, but it's not all bad. If you stay determined, you might find the right person this year.

Health

Your health might suffer this year due to heavy workload. No matter how important career is to you, being healthy is an integral part of doing your job well as well as your overall happiness. Cut yourself some slack from time to time so that you may continue to do your responsibilities with rejuvenated vigour.

Career

While you can do everything alone, it won't be as fulfilling or rewarding as working with other people. Try to make connections with others, be openminded with collaborating with them and enjoy the success together. Besides that, practice restrain with whatever resources available to ensure that your work is at an optimal level.

農曆正月

(February 4th - March 5th) 丙寅
You might feel like there's a lot to do this month but try to see where you are in the bigger picture. You have a choice not to work yourself into exhaustion just for the sake of getting things done.

農曆二月

(March 6th - April 4th) 丁卯
This month would be ideal for you to present your ideas to your colleagues and get their opinion on them, possibly opening doors for collaborations.

農曆三月

(April 5th - May 5th) 戊辰
You might be feeling lazier this month but don't let it get to you. As much as you'd like to let things be, you're going to live to regret not getting anything done later on.

農曆四月

(May 6th - June 5th) 己巳
There is possibility of injury to your legs this month. Be careful with any activity that involves using your legs such as sports or jogging. Besides that, pregnant women are also susceptible to potential accidents.

農曆五月

(June 6th - July 6th) 庚午
This month is good time for a fresh start. Don't be afraid to try new things or spice up old ideas. While your creativity is going strong, it will prime you up to be ready to tackle on any new challenge that might come your way.

農曆六月

(July 7th - August 7th) 辛未
Stress and fatigue will plague you this month. It will definitely affect multiple aspects of your life so it would be wise to do whatever it takes for you to minimize the negative effects.

農曆七月

(August 8th - September 7th) 壬申
Some financial problems might crop up this month. Get it settled as soon as possible, otherwise it might fester and metastasize into something worse.

農曆八月

(September 8th - October 7th) 癸酉
A series of unfortunate events will throw you off your game which in all likelihood pile more stress on you. These circumstances would make you irritable. With some self-awareness, you can control your emotions to a certain extent and keep your head cool.

農曆九月

(October 8th - November 7th) 甲戌
A project at work that's been facing many difficulties is finally near completion and with it comes the reward thanks to your part.

農曆十月

(November 8th - December 6th) 乙亥
You will be facing more workload this month. No matter the amount, stay calm and find it in you to strike the perfect balance between getting the job done and not let it deteriorate other aspects of your life.

農曆十一月

(December 7th 2019 - January 5th 2020) 丙子
A friend will say something to you this month that you will fail to understand and likely to offend you. When you're handling this, try to be more understanding so that you won't lose a friend over something that's not worth it.

農曆十二月

(January 6th - February 3rd 2020) 丁丑
There's a chance that certain individuals seek to hurt your reputation and thus circulate malicious rumours. Do your best to ignore them and simply move on with your life.

癸亥 Gui Hai Day

Overview

This year, your career might not be going anywhere and you feel like you have reached a dead end. It might be caused by the lack of strategy in dealing with your tasks or working with people who are not contributing as much as you are. Ideally, you should look for work that allows you to get away from it all and occupy your time on it.

Wealth

Wealth opportunities are plenty should you go for assignments that put you out of the country. For business owners, success will follow suit if you expand your business northwards or partner up with others. Make sure you are careful with your budget, save up more than you spend.

Relationships

It's a year of conflict for those in relationships. You might feel that you are neglected and this would turn to resentment towards your partner. These sorts of issues should be made clear to your significant other. For those not in a relationship, it would be best you don't get into one this year as it won't be worth the trouble.

Health

It is quite likely this year for you to gain much weight and in turn suffer from an increase in your blood cholesterol level. You really should be mindful with what you eat especially if it contains sugar. Start practicing healthy living habits as it will be better for you in the long run.

Career

It would be favourable for your career should you travel this year. New experience will grant you a fresh new outlook on things. Alternatively, you may consider moving up the corporate ladder or change departments. Getting out of your comfort zone will allow you to improve and advance in your career.

農曆正月

(February 4th - March 5th) 丙寅
Your superior will trust you with new tasks this month. You may rely on your colleagues to ensure the completion of these new responsibilities.

農曆二月

(March 6th - April 4th) 丁卯
Pay attention to what others has to say this month. Their advice may be beneficial for you in such a way that it is practical to apply.

農曆三月

(April 5th - May 5th) 戊辰
Procrastinating will only cause you more problems and stress in the future. Learn to schedule your work properly and avoid unnecessary distractions.

農曆四月

(May 6th - June 5th) 己巳
You might experience some stomach-related ailment this month. Seek medical treatment as soon as the symptoms appear.

農曆五月

(June 6th - July 6th) 庚午
Some people at work seek to take advantage of you by stealing your ideas. Make sure you choose who you trust your thought with carefully.

農曆六月

(July 7th - August 7th) 辛未
There's a chance that you're feeling stagnant at work and this would translate to frustration and demotivation at work. Try to consider what you have going well and change your mindset to focus more on the positivity.

農曆七月

(August 8th - September 7th) 壬申
Your wealth luck is looking up this month and as such, you can be prepared to gain more rewards than usual.

農曆八月

(September 8th - October 7th) 癸酉
This month, it's possible that you would be swamped with work. This is where you have to know how to manage your workstyle so that you won't be dealing with a backlog of unfinished assigments near your deadline.

農曆九月

(October 8th - November 7th) 甲戌
It's a good time to go for a vacation in order to dispel all the stress you have been accumulating thus far.

農曆十月

(November 8th - December 6th) 乙亥
It would be favourable for you to travel north this month. Don't be afraid to try out new things or go to places you never been to.

農曆十一月

(December 7th 2019 - January 5th 2020) 丙子
Those in partnerships have to keep an eye out on their deal. There may be some unacceptable behaviour happening behind the scenes so transparency and accountability should be practiced.

農曆十二月

(January 6th - February 3rd 2020) 丁丑
You should spend more time with your loved ones this month. Make an effort to improve the relationship by being more honest and sincere with one another.

JOEY YAP's
QI MEN DUN JIA MASTERY PROGRAM

This is the world's most comprehensive training program on the subject of Qi Men Dun Jia. Joey Yap is the Qi Men Strategist for some of Asia's wealthiest tycoons. This program is modelled after Joey Yap's personal application methods, covering techniques and strategies he applies for his high net worth clients. There is a huge difference between studying the subject as a scholar and learning how to use it successfully as a Qi Men strategist. In this program, Joey Yap shares with you what he personally uses to transform his own life and the lives of million others. In other words, he shares with his students what actually works and not just what looks good in theory with no real practical value. This means that the program covers his personal trade secrets in using the art of Qi Men Dun Jia.

There are five unique programs, with each of them covering one specific application aspect of the Joey Yap's Qi Men Dun Jia system.

Joey Yap's training program focuses on getting results. Theories and formulas are provided in the course workbook so that valuable class time are not wasted dwelling on formulas. Each course comes with its own comprehensive 400-plus pages workbook. Taught once a year exclusively by Joey Yap, seats to these programs are extremely limited.

Getting Whatever You Want from Whatever You've Got™ Spiritual Qi Men™

Qi Men Forecasting Methods™

Qi Men Destiny & Life Transformation™

Qi Men Feng Shui™

Qi Men Strategic Execution™

Qi Men Warcraft™

Call +6(03) 2284 8080 or
email courses@masteryacademy.com for enquiries

JOEY YAP CONSULTING GROUP

Pioneering Metaphysics-Centric Personal and Corporate Consultations

Founded in 2002, the Joey Yap Consulting Group is the pioneer in the provision of metaphysics-driven coaching and consultation services for professionals and individuals alike. Under the leadership of the renowned international Chinese Metaphysics consultant, author and trainer, Dato' Joey Yap, it has become a world-class specialised metaphysics consulting firm with a strong presence in four continents, meeting the metaphysics-centric needs of its A-list clientele, ranging from celebrities to multinational corporations.

The Group's core consultation practice areas include Feng Shui, BaZi and Qi Men Dun Jia, which are complemented by ancillary services such as Date Selection, Face Reading and Yi Jing. Its team of highly trained professional consultants, led by its Chief Consultant, Dato' Joey Yap, is well-equipped with unparalleled knowledge and experience to help clients achieve their ultimate potentials in various fields and specialisations. Given its credentials, the Group is certainly the firm of choice across the globe for metaphysics-related consultations.

The Peerless Industry Expert

Benchmarked against the standards of top international consulting firms, our consultants work closely with our clients to achieve the best possible outcomes. The possibilities are infinite as our expertise extends from consultations related to the forces of nature under the subject of Feng Shui, to those related to Destiny Analysis and effective strategising under BaZi and Qi Men Dun Jia respectively.

To date, we have consulted a great diversity of clients, ranging from corporate clients – from various industries such as real estate, finance and telecommunication, amongst others – to the hundreds of thousands of individuals in their key life aspects. Adopting up-to-date and pragmatic approaches, we provide comprehensive services while upholding the importance of clients' priorities and effective outcomes. Recognised as the epitome of Chinese Metaphysics, we possess significant testimonies from worldwide clients as a trusted Brand.

Feng Shui Consultation

Residential Properties
- Initial Land/Property Assessment
- Residential Feng Shui Consultation
- Residential Land Selection
- End-to-End Residential Consultation

Commercial Properties
- Initial Land/Property Assessment
- Commercial Feng Shui Consultation
- Commercial Land Selection
- End-to-End Commercial Consultation

Property Developers
- End-to-End Consultation
- Post-Consultation Advisory Services
- Panel Feng Shui Consultant

Property Investors
- Your Personal Feng Shui Consultant
- Tailor-Made Packages

Memorial Parks & Burial Sites
- Yin House Feng Shui

BaZi Consultation

Personal Destiny Analysis
- Individual BaZi Analysis
- BaZi Analysis for Families

Strategic Analysis for Corporate Organizations
- BaZi Consultations for Corporations
- BaZi Analysis for Human Resource Management

Entrepreneurs and Business Owners
- BaZi Analysis for Entrepreneurs

Career Pursuits
- BaZi Career Analysis

Relationships
- Marriage and Compatibility Analysis
- Partnership Analysis

General Public
- Annual BaZi Forecast
- Your Personal BaZi Coach

Date Selection Consultation

- Marriage Date Selection
- Caesarean Birth Date Selection
- House-Moving Date Selection
- Renovation and Groundbreaking Dates
- Signing of Contracts
- O icial Openings
- Product Launches

Qi Men Dun Jia Consultation

Strategic Execution
- Business and Investment Prospects

Forecasting
- Wealth and Life Pursuits
- People and Environmental Matters

Feng Shui
- Residential Properties
- Commercial Properties

Speaking Engagement

Many reputable organisations and institutions have worked closely with Joey Yap Consulting Group to build a synergistic business relationship by engaging our team of consultants, which are led by Joey Yap, as speakers at their corporate events.

We tailor our seminars and talks to suit the anticipated or pertinent group of audience. Be it department subsidiary, your clients or even the entire corporation, we aim to fit your requirements in delivering the intended message(s) across.

CHINESE METAPHYSICS REFERENCE SERIES

The Chinese Metaphysics Reference Series is a collection of reference texts, source material, and educational textbooks to be used as supplementary guides by scholars, students, researchers, teachers and practitioners of Chinese Metaphysics.

These comprehensive and structured books provide fast, easy reference to aid in the study and practice of various Chinese Metaphysics subjects including Feng Shui, BaZi, Yi Jing, Zi Wei, Liu Ren, Ze Ri, Ta Yi, Qi Men Dun Jia and Mian Xiang.

The Chinese Metaphysics Compendium

At over 1,000 pages, the Chinese Metaphysics Compendium is a unique one-volume reference book that compiles ALL the formulas relating to Feng Shui, BaZi (Four Pillars of Destiny), Zi Wei (Purple Star Astrology), Yi Jing (I-Ching), Qi Men (Mystical Doorways), Ze Ri (Date Selection), Mian Xiang (Face Reading) and other sources of Chinese Metaphysics.

It is presented in the form of easy-to-read tables, diagrams and reference charts, all of which are compiled into one handy book. This first-of-its-kind compendium is presented in both English and its original Chinese language, so that none of the meanings and contexts of the technical terminologies are lost.

The only essential and comprehensive reference on Chinese Metaphysics, and an absolute must-have for all students, scholars, and practitioners of Chinese Metaphysics.

The Ten Thousand Year Calendar (Pocket Edition)	The Ten Thousand Year Calendar	Dong Gong Date Selection	The Date Selection Compendium	Plum Blossom Divination Reference Book	Xuan Kong Da Gua Ten Thousand Year Calendar	 San Yuan Dragon Gate Eight Formations Water Method
BaZi Hour Pillar Useful Gods - Wood	BaZi Hour Pillar Useful Gods - Fire	BaZi Hour Pillar Useful Gods - Earth	BaZi Hour Pillar Useful Gods - Metal	BaZi Hour Pillar Useful Gods - Water	Xuan Kong Da Gua Structures Reference Book	Xuan Kong Da Gua 64 Gua Transformation Analysis
BaZi Structures and Structural Useful Gods - Wood	BaZi Structures and Structural Useful Gods - Fire	BaZi Structures and Structural Useful Gods - Earth	BaZi Structures and Structural Useful Gods - Metal	BaZi Structures and Structural Useful Gods - Water	Earth Study Discern Truth Second Edition	Eight Mansions Bright Mirror
Secret of Xuan Kong	Ode to Flying Stars	Xuan Kong Purple White Script	Ode to Mysticism	The Yin House Handbook	Water Water Everywhere	Xuan Kong Da Gua Not Exactly For Dummies

Joey Yap's BaZi Profiling System

Three Levels of BaZi Profiling (English & Chinese versions)

In BaZi Profiling, there are three levels that reflect three different stages of a person's personal nature and character structure.

Level 1 – The Day Master

The Day Master in a nutshell is the basic you. The inborn personality. It is your essential character. It answers the basic question "who am I". There are ten basic personality profiles – the ten Day Masters – each with its unique set of personality traits, likes and dislikes.

Level 2 – The Structure

The Structure is your behavior and attitude – in other words, it is about how you use your personality. It expands on the Day Master (Level 1). The structure reveals your natural tendencies in life – are you a controller, creator, supporter, thinker or connector? Each of the Ten Day Masters express themselves differently through the five Structures. Why do we do the things we do? Why do we like the things we like? The answers are in our BaZi Structure.

Level 3 – The Profile

The Profile depicts your role in your life. There are ten roles (Ten BaZi Profiles) related to us. As to each to his or her own - the roles we play are different from one another and it is unique to each Profile.

What success means to you, for instance, differs from your friends – this is similar to your sense of achievement or whatever you think of your purpose in life is.

Through the BaZi Profile, you will learn the deeper level of your personality. It helps you become aware of your personal strengths and works as a trigger for you to make all the positive changes to be a better version of you.

Keep in mind, only through awareness that you will be able to maximise your natural talents, abilities and skills. Only then, ultimately, you will get to enter into what we refer as 'flow' of life – a state where you have the powerful force to naturally succeed in life.

www.BaZiprofiling.com

THE BaZi
60 PILLARS SERIES

The BaZi 60 Pillars Series is a collection of ten volumes focusing on each of the Pillars or Jia Zi in BaZi Astrology. Learn how to see BaZi Chart in a new light through the Pictorial Method of BaZi analysis and elevate your proficiency in BaZi studies through this new understanding. Joey Yap's 60 Pillars Life Analysis Method is a refined and enhanced technique that is based on the fundamentals set by the true masters of olden times, and modified to fit to the sophistication of current times.

BaZi Collection

With these books, leading Chinese Astrology Master Trainer Joey Yap makes it easy to learn how to unlock your Destiny through your BaZi. BaZi or Four Pillars of Destiny is an ancient Chinese science which enables individuals to understand their personality, hidden talents and abilities, as well as their luck cycle - by examining the information contained within their birth data.

Understand and learn more about this accurate ancient science with this BaZi Collection.

BOOK 1   BOOK 2   BOOK 3   BOOK 4   BOOK 5   The 10 Gods

(Available in English & Chinese)

Feng Shui Collection

Design Your Legacy

Design Your Legacy is Joey Yap's first book on the profound subject of Yin House Feng Shui, which is the study Feng Shui for burials and tombs. Although it is still pretty much a hidden practice that is largely unexplored by modern literature, the significance of Yin House Feng Shui has permeated through the centuries – from the creation of the imperial lineage of emperors in ancient times to the iconic leaders who founded modern China.

This book unveils the true essence of Yin House Feng Shui with its significant applications that are unlike the myths and superstition which have for years, overshadowed the genuine practice itself. Discover how Yin House Feng Shui – the true precursor to all modern Feng Shui practice, can be used to safeguard the future of your descendants and create a lasting legacy.

Must-Haves for Property Analysis!

For homeowners, those looking to build their own home or even investors who are looking to apply Feng Shui to their homes, these series of books provides valuable information from the classical Feng Shui therioes and applications.

In his trademark straight-to-the-point manner, Joey shares with you the Feng Shui do's and dont's when it comes to finding a property with favorable Feng Shui, which is condusive for home living.

Stories and Lessons on Feng Shui Series

All in all, this series is a delightful chronicle of Joey's articles, thoughts and vast experience - as a professional Feng Shui consultant and instructor - that have been purposely refined, edited and expanded upon to make for a light-hearted, interesting yet educational read. And with Feng Shui, BaZi, Mian Xiang and Yi Jing all thrown into this one dish, there's something for everyone.

(Available in English & Chinese)

More Titles under Joey Yap Books

Pure Feng Shui

Pure Feng Shui is Joey Yap's debut with an international publisher, CICO Books. It is a refreshing and elegant look at the intricacies of Classical Feng Shui - now compiled in a useful manner for modern day readers. This book is a comprehensive introduction to all the important precepts and techniques of Feng Shui practices.

Your Aquarium Here

This book is the first in Fengshuilogy Series, which is a series of matter-of-fact and useful Feng Shui books designed for the person who wants to do a fuss-free Feng Shui.

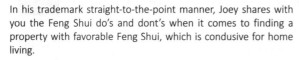

More Titles under Joey Yap Books

Walking the Dragons

Compiled in one book for the first time from Joey Yap's Feng Shui Mastery Excursion Series, the book highlights China's extensive, vibrant history with astute observations on the Feng Shui of important sites and places. Learn the landform formations of Yin Houses (tombs and burial places), as well as mountains, temples, castles and villages.

Walking the Dragons : Taiwan Excursion

A Guide to Classical Landform Feng Shui of Taiwan

From China to Tibet, Joey Yap turns his analytical eye towards Taiwan in this extensive Walking the Dragons series. Combined with beautiful images and detailed information about an island once known as Formosa, or "Beautiful Island" in Portuguese, this compelling series of essays highlights the colourful history and wonders of Taiwan. It also provides readers with fascinating insights into the living science of Feng Shui.

The Art of Date Selection: Personal Date Selection (Available in English & Chinese)

With the Art of Date Selection: Personal Date Selection, you can learn simple, practical methods to select not just good dates, but personalised good dates as well. Whether it is a personal activity such as a marriage or professional endeavour, such as launching a business - signing a contract or even acquiring assets, this book will show you how to pick the good dates and tailor them to suit the activity in question, and to avoid the negative ones too!

Your Head Here

Your Head Here is the first book by Sherwin Ng. She is an accomplished student of Joey Yap, and an experienced Feng Shui consultant and instructor with Joey Yap Consulting Group and Mastery Academy respectively. It is the second book under the Fengshuilogy series, which focuses on Bedroom Feng Shui, a specific topic dedicated to optimum bed location and placement.

If the Shoe Fits

This book is for those who want to make the effort to enhance their relationship.

In her debut release, Jessie Lee humbly shares with you the classical BaZi method of the Ten Day Masters and the combination of a new profiling system developed by Joey Yap, to understand and deal with the people around you.

Being Happy and Successful at Work and in your Career

Have you ever wondered why some of us are so successful in our careers while others are dragging their feet to work or switching from one job to another? Janet Yung hopes to answer this question by helping others through the knowledge and application of BaZi and Chinese Astrology. In her debut release, she shares with the readers the right way of using BaZi to understand themselves: their inborn talents, motivations, skills, and passions, to find their own place in the path of professional development.

Being Happy & Successful - Managing Yourself & Others

Manage Your Talent & Have Effective Relationships at the Workplace

While many strive for efficiency in the workplace, it is vital to know how to utilize your talents. In this book, Janet Yung will take you further on how to use the BaZi profiling system as a tool to assess your personality and understanding your approach to the job. From ways in communicating with your colleagues to understanding your boss, you will be astounded by what this ancient system can reveal about you and the people in your life. Tips and guidance will also be given in this book so that you will make better decisions for your next step in advancing in your career.

The BaZi Road to Success

The BaZi Road to Success explains your journey in life through a chart that is obtained just from looking at the date you were born and its connection with key BaZi elements.

Your Day Pillar, Hour Pillar, Luck Pillar and Annual Pillar all come together to paint a BaZi chart that churns out a combination of different elements, which the book helps interpret. From relationships, career advice, future plans and possibility of wealth accumulation - this book covers it all!

The Chinese Art of Face Reading: The Book of Moles

The Book of Moles by Joey Yap delves into the inner meanings of moles and what they reveal about the personality and destiny of an individual. Complemented by fascinating illustrations and Joey Yap's easy-to-understand commentaries and guides, this book takes a deeper focus into a Face Reading subject, which can be used for everyday decisions – from personal relationships to professional dealings and many others.

Discover Face Reading (Available in English & Chinese)

This is a comprehensive book on all areas of Face Reading, covering some of the most important facial features, including the forehead, mouth, ears and even philtrum above your lips. This book will help you analyse not just your Destiny but also help you achieve your full potential and achieve life fulfillment.

Joey Yap's Art of Face Reading

The Art of Face Reading is Joey Yap's second effort with CICO Books, and it takes a lighter, more practical approach to Face Reading. This book does not focus on the individual features as it does on reading the entire face. It is about identifying common personality types and characters.

Faces of Fortune 2

We don't need to go far to look for entrepreneurs with the X-Factor. Malaysia produces some of the best entrepreneurs in the world. In this book, we will tell you the rags-to-riches stories of 9 ordinary people who has no special privileges, and how they made it on their own.

Easy Guide on Face Reading (Available in English & Chinese)

The Face Reading Essentials series of books comprises of five individual books on the key features of the face – the Eyes, the Eyebrows, the Ears, the Nose, and the Mouth. Each book provides a detailed illustration and a simple yet descriptive explanation on the individual types of the features.

The books are equally useful and effective for beginners, enthusiasts and those who are curious. The series is designed to enable people who are new to Face Reading to make the most out of first impressions and learn to apply Face Reading skills to understand the personality and character of their friends, family, co-workers and business associates.

2019 Annual Releases

Chinese Astrology for 2019	Feng Shui for 2019	Tong Shu Desktop Calendar 2019	Qi Men Desktop Calendar 2019	Professional Tong Shu Diary 2019	Tong Shu Monthly Planner 2019	Weekly Tong Shu Diary 2019

Cultural Series

Discover the True Significance of the Ancient Art of Lion Dance

The Lion has long been a symbol of power and strength. That powerful symbol has evolved into an incredible display of a mixture of martial arts and ritualism that is the Lion Dance. Throughout ancient and modern times, the Lion Dance has stamped itself as a popular part of culture, but is there a meaning lost behind this magnificent spectacle?

The Art of Lion Dance written by the world's number one man in Chinese Metaphysics, Dato' Joey Yap, explains the history and origins of the art and its connection to Qi Men Dun Jia. By creating that bridge with Qi Men, the Lion Dance is able to ritualise any type of ceremony, celebrations and mourning alike.

The book is the perfect companion to the modern interpretation of the art as it reveals the significance behind each part of the Lion costume, as well as rituals that are put in place to bring the costume and its spectacle to life.

Chinese Traditions & Practices

China has a long, rich history spanning centuries. As Chinese culture has evolved over the centuries, so have the country's many customs and traditions. Today, there's a Chinese custom for just about every important event in a person's life — from cradle to the grave.

Although many China's customs have survived to the present day, some have been all but forgotten: rendered obsolete by modern day technology. This book explores the history of Chinese traditions and cultural practices, their purpose, and the differences between the traditions of the past and their modern incarnations.

If you are a westerner or less informed about Chinese culture, you may find this book particularly useful, especially when it comes to doing business with the Chinese — whether it be in China itself or some other country with a considerable Chinese population. If anything, it will allow you to have a better casual understanding of the culture and traditions of your Chinese friends or acquaintances. An understanding of Chinese traditions leads to a more informed, richer appreciation of Chinese culture and China itself.

Educational Tools and Software

Joey Yap's Feng Shui Template Set

Directions are the cornerstone of any successful Feng Shui audit or application. The Joey Yap Feng Shui Template Set is a set of three templates to simplify the process of taking directions and determining locations and positions, whether it is for a building, a house, or an open area such as a plot of land - all of it done with just a floor plan or area map.

The Set comprises three basic templates: The Basic Feng Shui Template, Eight Mansions Feng Shui Template, and the Flying Stars Feng Shui Template.

Mini Feng Shui Compass

The Mini Feng Shui Compass is a self-aligning compass that is not only light at 100gms but also built sturdily to ensure it will be convenient to use anywhere. The rings on the Mini Feng Shui Compass are bilingual and incorporate the 24 Mountain Rings that is used in your traditional Luo Pan.

The comprehensive booklet included with this, will guide you in applying the 24 Mountain Directions on your Mini Feng Shui Compass effectively and the Eight Mansions Feng Shui to locate the most auspicious locations within your home, office and surroundings. You can also use the Mini Feng Shui Compass when measuring the direction of your property for the purpose of applying Flying Stars Feng Shui.

MASTERY ACADEMY
OF CHINESE METAPHYSICS
Your **Preferred** Choice to the Art & Science of
Classical Chinese Metaphysics Studies

Bringing **innovative** techniques and **creative** teaching methods to an ancient study.

Mastery Academy of Chinese Metaphysics was established by Joey Yap to play the role of disseminating this Eastern knowledge to the modern world with the belief that this valuable knowledge should be accessible to everyone and everywhere.

Its goal is to enrich people's lives through accurate, professional teaching and practice of Chinese Metaphysics knowledge globally. It is the first academic institution of its kind in the world to adopt the tradition of Western institutions of higher learning - where students are encouraged to explore, question and challenge themselves, as well as to respect different fields and branches of studies. This is done together with the appreciation and respect of classical ideas and applications that have stood the test of time.

The Art and Science of Chinese Metaphysics — be it Feng Shui, BaZi (Astrology), Qi Men Dun Jia, Mian Xiang (Face Reading), ZeRi (Date Selection) or Yi Jing — is no longer a field shrouded with mystery and superstition. In light of new technology, fresher interpretations and innovative methods, as well as modern teaching tools like the Internet, interactive learning, e-learning and distance learning, anyone from virtually any corner of the globe, who is keen to master these disciplines can do so with ease and confidence under the guidance and support of the Academy.

It has indeed proven to be a centre of educational excellence for thousands of students from over thirty countries across the world; many of whom have moved on to practice classical Chinese Metaphysics professionally in their home countries.

At the Academy, we believe in enriching people's lives by empowering their destinies through the disciplines of Chinese Metaphysics. Learning is not an option - it is a way of life!

MASTERY ACADEMY
OF CHINESE METAPHYSICS™

MALAYSIA
19-3, The Boulevard, Mid Valley City, 59200 Kuala Lumpur, Malaysia
Tel : +6(03)-2284 8080 | Fax : +6(03)-2284 1218
Email   : info@masteryacademy.com
Website : www.masteryacademy.com

Australia, Austria, Canada, China, Croatia, Cyprus, Czech Republic, Denmark, France, Germany, Greece, Hungary, India, Italy, Kazakhstan, Malaysia, Netherlands (Holland), New Zealand, Philippines, Poland, Russian Federation, Singapore, Slovenia, South Africa, Switzerland, Turkey, United States of America, Ukraine, United Kingdom

The Mastery Academy around the world!

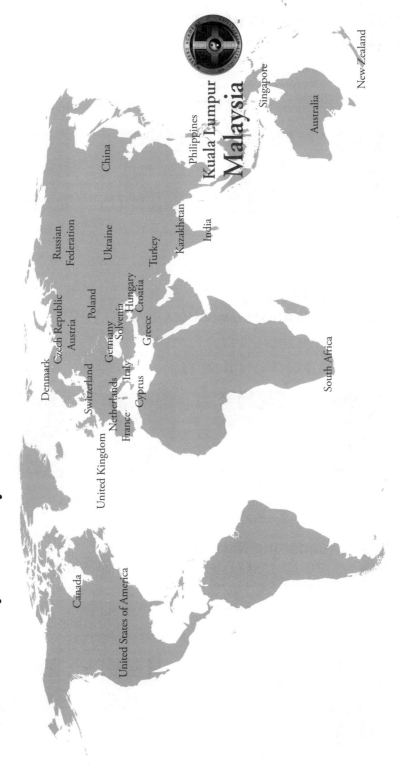

Feng Shui Mastery™
LIVE COURSES (MODULES ONE TO FOUR)

This an ideal program for those who wants to achieve mastery in Feng Shui from the comfort of their homes. This comprehensive program covers the foundation up to the advanced practitioner levels, touching upon the important theories from various classical Feng Shui systems including Ba Zhai, San Yuan, San He and Xuan Kong.

Module One:
Beginners
Course

Module Two:
Practitioners
Course

Module Three:
Advanced
Practitioners Course

Module Four:
Master Course

BaZi Mastery™
LIVE COURSES (MODULES ONE TO FOUR)

This lesson-based program brings a thorough introduction to BaZi and guides the student step-by-step, all the way to the professional practitioner level. From the theories to the practical, BaZi students along with serious Feng Shui practitioners, can master its application with accuracy and confidence.

Module One:
Intensive
Foundation Course

Module Two:
Practitioners
Course

Module Three:
Advanced
Practitioners Course

Module Four:
Master Course in BaZi

Xuan Kong Mastery™
LIVE COURSES (MODULES ONE TO THREE)
* Advanced Courses For Master Practitioners

Xuan Kong is a sophisticated branch of Feng Shui, replete with many techniques and formulae, which encompass numerology, symbology and the science of the Ba Gua, along with the mathematics of time. This program is ideal for practitioners looking to bring their practice to a more in-depth level.

Module One:
Advanced
Foundation Course

Module Two A:
Advanced Xuan
Kong Methodologies

Module Two B:
Purple White

Module Three:
Advanced Xuan Kong
Da Gua

Mian Xiang Mastery™
LIVE COURSES (MODULES ONE AND TWO)

This program comprises of two modules, each carefully developed to allow students to familiarise with the fundamentals of Mian Xiang or Face Reading and the intricacies of its theories and principles. With lessons guided by video lectures, presentations and notes, students are able to understand and practice Mian Xiang with greater depth.

Module One:
Basic Face Reading

Module Two:
Practical Face Reading

Yi Jing Mastery™
LIVE COURSES (MODULES ONE AND TWO)

Whether you are a casual or serious Yi Jing enthusiast, this lesson-based program contains two modules that brings students deeper into the Chinese science of divination. The lessons will guide students on the mastery of its sophisticated formulas and calculations to derive answers to questions we pose.

Module One:
Traditional Yi Jing

Module Two:
Plum Blossom Numerology

Ze Ri Mastery™
LIVE COURSES (MODULES ONE AND TWO)

In two modules, students will undergo a thorough instruction on the fundamentals of ZeRi or Date Selection. The comprehensive program covers Date Selection for both Personal and Feng Shui purposes to Xuan Kong Da Gua Date Selection.

Module One:
Personal and Feng Shui Date Selection

Module Two:
Xuan Kong Da Gua Date Selection

Joey Yap's
SAN YUAN QI MEN XUAN KONG DA GUA™

This is an advanced level program which can be summed up as the Integral Vision of San Yuan studies – an integration of the ancient potent discipline of Qi Men Dun Jia and the highly popular Xuan Kong 64 Hexagrams. Often regarded as two independent systems, San Yuan Qi Men and San Yuan Xuan Kong Da Gua can trace their origins to the same source and were actually used together in ancient times by great Chinese sages.

This method enables practitioners to harness the Qi of time and space, and predict the outcomes through a highly-detailed analysis of landforms, places and sites.

BaZi 10X

Emphasising on the practical aspects of BaZi, this programme is rich with numerous applications and techniques pertaining to the pursuit of wealth, health, relationship and career, all of which constitute the formula of success. This programme is designed for all levels of practitioners and is supplemented with innovative learning materials to enable easy learning. Discover the different layers of BaZi from a brand new perspective with BaZi 10X.

Feng Shui for Life

This is an entry-level five-day course designed for the Feng Shui beginner to learn the application of practical Feng Shui in day-to-day living. Lessons include quick tips on analysing the BaZi chart, simple Feng Shui solutions for the home, basic Date Selection, useful Face Reading techniques and practical Water formulas. A great introduction course on Chinese Metaphysics studies for beginners.

Joey Yap's
Design Your Destiny

This is a three-day life transformation program designed to inspire awareness and action for you to create a better quality of life. It introduces the DRT™ (Decision Referential Technology) method, which utilises the BaZi Personality Profiling system to determine the right version of you, and serves as a tool to help you make better decisions and achieve a better life in the least resistant way possible, based on your Personality Profile Type.

Millionaire Feng Shui Secrets Programme

This program is geared towards maximising your financial goals and dreams through the use of Feng Shui. Focusing mainly on the execution of Wealth Feng Shui techniques such as Luo Shu sectors and more, it is perfect for boosting careers, businesses and investment opportunities.

Grow Rich With BaZi Programme

This comprehensive programme covers the foundation of BaZi studies and presents information from the career, wealth and business standpoint. This course is ideal for those who want to maximise their wealth potential and live the life they deserve. Knowledge gained in this course will be used as driving factors to encourage personal development towards a better future.

Walk the Mountains!
Learn Feng Shui in a Practical and Hands-on Program

 ## Feng Shui Mastery Excursion™

Learn landform (Luan Tou) Feng Shui by walking the mountains and chasing the Dragon's vein in China. This program takes the students in a study tour to examine notable Feng Shui landmarks, mountains, hills, valleys, ancient palaces, famous mansions, houses and tombs in China. The excursion is a practical hands-on course where students are shown to perform readings using the formulas they have learnt and to recognise and read Feng Shui Landform (Luan Tou) formations.

Read about the China Excursion here:
http://www.fengshuiexcursion.com

Mastery Academy courses are conducted around the world. Find out when will Joey Yap be in your area by visiting
www.masteryacademy.com
or call our offices at **+6(03)-2284 8080**.

Online Home Study Courses

Gain Valuable Knowledge from the Comfort of Your Home

Now, armed with your trusty computer or laptop and Internet access, the knowledge of Chinese Metaphysics is just a click away!

3 Easy Steps to Activate Your Home Study Course:

Step 1:
Go to the URL as indicated on the Activation Card and key in your Activation Code

Step 2:
At the Registration page, fill in the details accordingly to enable us to generate your Student Identification (Student ID).

Step 3:
Upon successful registration, you may begin your lessons immediately.

Joey Yap's Feng Shui Mastery HomeStudy Course

Module 1: Empowering Your Home
Module 2: Master Practitioner Program

Learn how easy it is to harness the power of the environment to promote health, wealth and prosperity in your life. The knowledge and applications of Feng Shui will not be a mystery but a valuable tool you can master on your own.

Joey Yap's BaZi Mastery HomeStudy Course

Module 1: Mapping Your Life
Module 2: Mastering Your Future

Discover your path of least resistance to success with insights about your personality and capabilities, and what strengths you can tap on to maximise your potential for success and happiness by mastering BaZi (Chinese Astrology). This course will teach you all the essentials you need to interpret a BaZi chart and more.

Joey Yap's Mian Xiang Mastery HomeStudy Course

Module 1: Face Reading
Module 2: Advanced Face Reading

A face can reveal so much about a person. Now, you can learn the Art and Science of Mian Xiang (Chinese Face Reading) to understand a person's character based on his or her facial features, with ease and confidence.